$\mathscr{P}$ROFILES IN WORLD HISTORY

Significant Events and the People Who Shaped Them

Volume 3: *The Crusades to Building Empires in the Americas, 1095-1500*

Crusades and Mongol Expansion
Saladin, Genghis Khan, Innocent III, Alexius V
Religion and Reason in the Middle Ages
Averroës, Maimonides, Thomas Aquinas
Beginning of Constitutional Government in England
Thomas Becket, King John
Muslim Influences on Empires in West Africa
Al-Bakri, Sundiata, Mansa Musa
Exploring the East
Marco Polo, William of Rubrouck, Ibn Battutah
Building Empires in Europe and Asia
Timur Lenk, Mehmed II, Ivan the Great, Babur
Building Empires in the Americas
Topa Inca Yupanqui, Moctezuma I

Volume 4: *The Age of Discovery to Industrial Revolution, 1400-1830*

Beginnings of the Age of Discovery
Cheng Ho, Vasco da Gama, Jacques Cartier
Religious Reform
Desiderius Erasmus, Guru Nanak, Ignatius of Loyola, Martin Luther
Revival of Science
Leonardo da Vinci, Tycho Brahe, Johannes Kepler
Revival of Literature
Francis Bacon, Miguel de Cervantes, William Shakespeare
Rise of Nationalism
Suleiman the Magnificent, Hideyoshi Toyotomi, Catherine the Great
Enlightenment
John Locke, Voltaire, Jean-Jacques Rousseau
Industrial Revolution
Charles Townshend, Richard Arkwright, James Watt

(Contin d on in

PROFILES IN
WORLD HISTORY

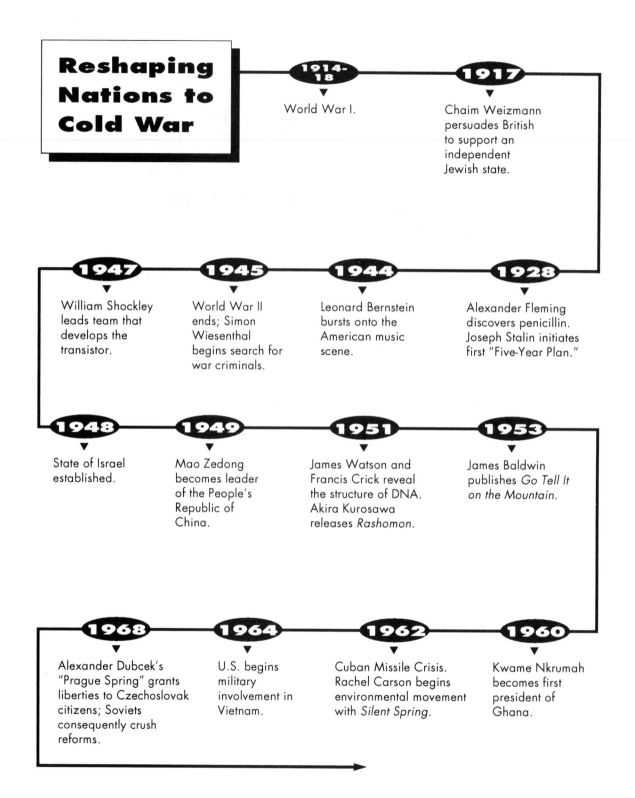

Reshaping Nations to Cold War

1914-18
World War I.

1917
Chaim Weizmann persuades British to support an independent Jewish state.

1928
Alexander Fleming discovers penicillin. Joseph Stalin initiates first "Five-Year Plan."

1944
Leonard Bernstein bursts onto the American music scene.

1945
World War II ends; Simon Wiesenthal begins search for war criminals.

1947
William Shockley leads team that develops the transistor.

1948
State of Israel established.

1949
Mao Zedong becomes leader of the People's Republic of China.

1951
James Watson and Francis Crick reveal the structure of DNA. Akira Kurosawa releases *Rashomon*.

1953
James Baldwin publishes *Go Tell It on the Mountain*.

1960
Kwame Nkrumah becomes first president of Ghana.

1962
Cuban Missile Crisis. Rachel Carson begins environmental movement with *Silent Spring*.

1964
U.S. begins military involvement in Vietnam.

1968
Alexander Dubcek's "Prague Spring" grants liberties to Czechoslovak citizens; Soviets consequently crush reforms.

PROFILES IN WORLD HISTORY

Significant Events and the People Who Shaped Them

Reshaping Nations to Cold War

JOYCE MOSS
and
GEORGE WILSON

AN IMPRINT OF GALE RESEARCH
AN INTERNATIONAL THOMSON PUBLISHING COMPANY

PROFILES IN WORLD HISTORY

Significant Events and the People Who Shaped Them

VOLUME 7: RESHAPING NATIONS TO COLD WAR

Joyce Moss and George Wilson

Staff

Carol DeKane Nagel, *U•X•L Developmental Editor*
Julie L. Carnagie, *U•X•L Assistant Editor*
Thomas L. Romig, *U•X•L Publisher*

Shanna P. Heilveil, *Production Assistant*
Evi Seoud, *Assistant Production Manager*
Mary Beth Trimper, *Production Director*

Barbara A. Wallace, *Permissions Associate (Pictures)*

Mary Krzewinski, *Cover and Page Designer*
Cynthia Baldwin, *Art Director*

The Graphix Group, *Typesetting*

∞™ This book is printed on acid-free paper that meets the minimum requirements of American National Standard for Information Sciences—Permanence Paper for Printed Library Materials, ANSI Z39.48-1984.

ISBN 0-7876-0464-X (Set)
ISBN 0-7876-0465-8 (v. 1)
ISBN 0-7876-0466-6 (v. 2)
ISBN 0-7876-0467-4 (v. 3)
ISBN 0-7876-0468-2 (v. 4)
ISBN 0-7876-0469-0 (v. 5)
ISBN 0-7876-0470-4 (v. 6)
ISBN 0-7876-0471-2 (v. 7)
ISBN 0-7876-0472-0 (v. 8)

Printed in the United States of America

I⟨T⟩P™   U·X·L is an imprint of Gale Research,
an International Thomson Publishing Company.
ITP logo is a trademark under license.

Contents

Reshaping European and Asian Nations   1

Ending Imperialism   36

Preserving the Jewish Identity   76

Breakthoughs in Science and Technology   110

Expanding the Humanities   144

Cold War   172

Reader's Guide

Profiles in World History: Significant Events and the People Who Shaped Them presents the life stories of more than 175 individuals who have played key roles in world history. The biographies are clustered around 50 broad events, ranging from the Rise of Eastern Religions and Philosophies to the Expansion of World Powers, from Industrial Revolution to Winning African Independence. Each biography—complete in itself—contributes a singular outlook regarding an event; when taken as cluster, the biographies provide a variety of views and experiences, thereby offering a broad perspective on events that shaped the world.

Those whose stories are told in *Profiles in World History* meet one or more of the following criteria. The individuals:

- Represent viewpoints or groups involved in a major world event
- Directly affected the outcome of the event
- Exemplify a role played by common citizens in that event

Format

Profiles in World History volumes are arranged by chapter. Each chapter focuses on one particular event and opens with an overview and detailed time line of the event that places it in historical context. Following are biographical profiles of two to five diverse individuals who played active roles in the event.

Each biographical profile is divided into four sections:

- **Personal Background** provides details that predate and anticipate the individual's involvement in the event

- **Participation** describes the role played by the individual in the event and its impact on his or her life

- **Aftermath** discusses effects of the individual's actions and subsequent relevant events in the person's life

- **For More Information** provides sources for further reading on the individual

Additionally, sidebars containing interesting details about the events and individuals profiled are interspersed throughout the text.

Additional Features

Portraits, illustrations, and maps as well as excerpts from primary source materials are included in *Profiles in World History* to help bring history to life. Sources of all quoted material are cited parenthetically within the text, and complete bibliographic information is listed at the end of each biography. A full bibliography of scholarly sources consulted in preparing each volume appears in each book's back matter.

Cross references are made in the entries, directing readers to other entries within the volume that are connected in some way to the person under scrutiny. Additionally, each volume ends with a subject index, while Volume 8 concludes with a cumulative subject index, providing easy access to the people and events mentioned throughout *Profiles in World History.*

Comments and Suggestions

We welcome your comments on this work as well as your suggestions for individuals to be featured in future editions of *Profiles in World History.* Please write: Editors, *Profiles in World History,* U·X·L, 835 Penobscot Bldg., Detroit, Michigan 48226-4094; fax to 313-961-6348; or call toll-free: 1-800-877-4253.

Acknowledgments

The editors would like to thank the many people involved in the preparation of *Profiles in World History*.

For guidance in the choice of events and personalities, we are grateful to Ross Dunn, Professor of History at the University of California at San Diego, and David Smith, Professor of History at California Polytechnic University at Pomona. We're thankful to Professor Smith for his careful review of the entire series and his guidance toward key sources of information about personalities and events.

We deeply appreciate the writers who compiled data and contributed to the biographies: Diane Ahrens, Bill Boll, Quesiyah Ali Chavez, Charity-Jean Conklin, Mario Cutajar, Craig Hinkel, Hillary Manning, Lawrence Orr, Phillip T. Slattery, Colin Wells, and Susan Yun. We'd especially like to thank Jamie Mohn and Cheryl Steets for their careful attention to the manuscript.

Thanks also to the copy editors and proofreaders, Sonia Benson, Barbara C. Bigelow, Betz Des Chenes, Robert Griffin, Rob Nagel, and Paulette Petrimoulx, for their careful attention to style and detail. Special thanks to Margaret M. Johnson, Judith Kass, and John F. Petruccione for researching the illustrations and maps.

And, finally, thanks to Carol Nagel of U·X·L for overseeing the production of the series.

Picture Credits

The photographs and illustrations appearing in *Profiles in World History: Significant Events and the People Who Shaped Them,* Volume 7: *Reshaping Nations to Cold War* were received from the following sources:

On the cover: Ho Chi Minh; **The Granger Collection:** Golda Meir, Jawaharlal Nehru.

AP/Wide World Photos: pp. 61, 66, 105, 123, 141, 146, 167, 189, 191, 212; **Archive Photos:** pp. 41, 103, 139; **Archive Photos/Interfoto/MTI:** p. 53; **The Bettmann Archive:** pp. 115, 158, 162, 177, 179; **The Granger Collection:** pp. 3, 5, 15, 18, 22, 26, 29, 55, 74, 84, 91, 120, 129, 165, 181, 199; **Orion Classics:** p. 154; **Reuters/Bettmann:** pp. 106, 149, 197; **Toko Films:** p. 152; **United Nations:** p. 187; **UPI/Bettmann:** pp. 7, 25, 31, 47, 81, 86, 97, 137, 203, 207, 210; **UPI/Bettmann Newsphotos:** pp. 73, 101.

Reshaping European and Asian Nations

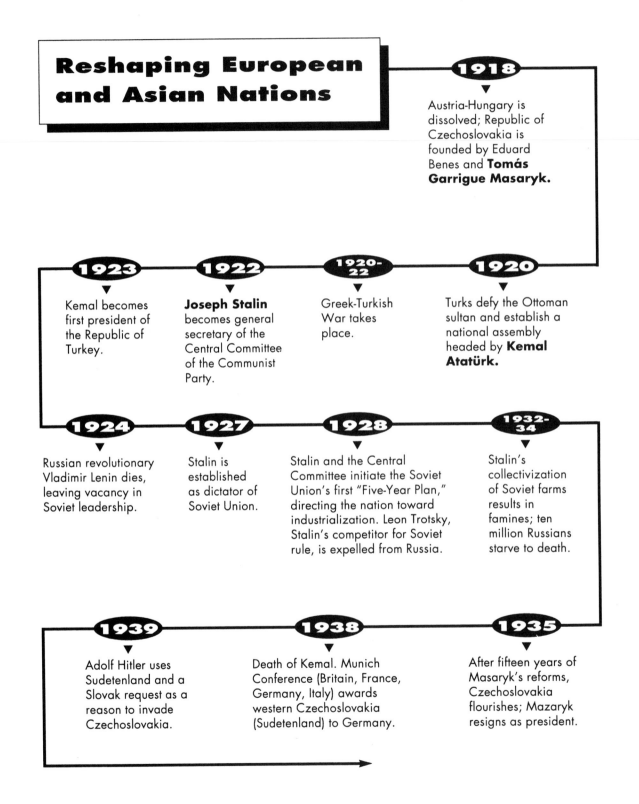

1918
Austria-Hungary is dissolved; Republic of Czechoslovakia is founded by Eduard Benes and **Tomás Garrigue Masaryk.**

1920
Turks defy the Ottoman sultan and establish a national assembly headed by **Kemal Atatürk.**

1920-22
Greek-Turkish War takes place.

1922
Joseph Stalin becomes general secretary of the Central Committee of the Communist Party.

1923
Kemal becomes first president of the Republic of Turkey.

1924
Russian revolutionary Vladimir Lenin dies, leaving vacancy in Soviet leadership.

1927
Stalin is established as dictator of Soviet Union.

1928
Stalin and the Central Committee initiate the Soviet Union's first "Five-Year Plan," directing the nation toward industrialization. Leon Trotsky, Stalin's competitor for Soviet rule, is expelled from Russia.

1932-34
Stalin's collectivization of Soviet farms results in famines; ten million Russians starve to death.

1935
After fifteen years of Masaryk's reforms, Czechoslovakia flourishes; Mazaryk resigns as president.

1938
Death of Kemal. Munich Conference (Britain, France, Germany, Italy) awards western Czechoslovakia (Sudetenland) to Germany.

1939
Adolf Hitler uses Sudetenland and a Slovak request as a reason to invade Czechoslovakia.

RESHAPING EUROPEAN AND ASIAN NATIONS

World War I radically altered the map of Europe as the victorious Allied forces searched for an alignment that would produce a permanent peace. Three great European empires—Austria-Hungary, Germany, and Russia—virtually disappeared, and a fourth, Turkey's Ottoman empire, soon followed. Germany and Turkey became republics, Russia was transformed into a communist dictatorship, and the Austro-Hungarian empire was divided into the independent nations of Austria and Hungary. Seven new nations emerged in Eastern Europe following the breakup of these empires.

As nations were split apart and new ones created, an intense ideological struggle began. In the last quarter of the nineteenth century, a German revolutionary named Karl Marx had offered an alternative to capitalism (an economic system of private ownership, often by a ruling elite class). He is remembered in history as the founder of modern communism (the realization of a classless society marked by communal ownership of all property). To many poor and sometimes starving peasants in the middle European empires, Marx's ideas seemed to hold great promise. The struggle for communism ran through Europe and finally overthrew capitalism in the remains of the old Russian empire. Meanwhile, other students of government and economics were working toward the creation of greater equality and productivity, using the capitalist system of the United States as a model.

Czechoslovakia. One of the new nations was Czechoslovakia, which owed its independence, in a large part, to the efforts of **Tomás Garrigue Masaryk,** a university professor. He became a spokesperson for the Czech people within the Austro-Hungarian empire. While in exile during World War I, Masaryk led the fight for Czechoslovakia's independence and eventually became the nation's first president. Under his leadership, Czechoslovakia became a constitutional republic.

Turkey. The son of a minor government official, Turkish politician **Kemal Atatürk** embarked upon a military career and became a war hero. After the Ottoman empire collapsed at the end of World War I, he organized a nationalist rebellion to assert Turkish independence. An authoritarian ruler, Kemal tried to transform Turkey into a modern westernized nation.

The Soviet Union. The Soviet Union was a huge federation of republics that spanned from eastern Europe through northern Asia. **Joseph Stalin,** the son of a poor Georgian shoemaker, became a professional revolutionary and a leading Bolshevik. (Bolsheviks were Russian revolutionaries who led the Russian Revolution of 1917, which resulted in the formation of the communist Soviet state.) Following the death of Bolshevik leader Vladimir Lenin, Stalin maneuvered his way into becoming absolute ruler of the Soviet Union. Having gained total power, he launched a program of rapid industrialization and collectivized (or communal, state-controlled) agriculture. He also conducted a series of purges to rid the Communist Party of its alleged enemies. Stalin's policies resulted in the deaths of millions of people and transformed the economy and culture of the Soviet Union.

New European Nations After World War I

Out of World War I came the formation of Czechoslovakia, Estonia, Finland, Latvia, Lithuania, Poland, and Yugoslavia. In addition, the dual kingdom of Austria-Hungary was divided, and the three great central European empires lost territories and changed their forms of government.

▲ The ideas of nineteenth-century political philosopher Karl Marx
seemed to hold great promise. The struggle for communism ran
through Europe and finally overthrew capitalism in the remains of the
old Russian empire.

Tomás Garrigue Masaryk

1850-1937

Personal Background

Early life. Tomás Masaryk was born on March 7, 1850, in Hodonin, a village in the kingdom of Moravia, which was part of the Austrian (later Austro-Hungarian) empire. His father, who worked as a coachman on a large estate, was a former serf.

As a young man, Masaryk had a difficult time deciding what he wanted to do with his life. He attended private and religious schools and later worked as an apprentice to a locksmith in Vienna. But he soon grew to hate the monotonous routine and returned home, much to his father's displeasure. Masaryk was next employed as a blacksmith until his mother and one of his former teachers convinced him to return to school. Accordingly, he entered a secondary school in nearby Cejkovice and was soon serving as an instructor there.

Masaryk was expelled from the school for flirting with his landlady's sister and then not confessing his "sin" to the school chaplain. Just as he figured his educational opportunities had come to an end, his friend's father, Frantisek Le Monnier, was appointed chief of police for Vienna. Le Monnier allowed Masaryk to use his extensive library. The eager young student became acquainted with great literature and became increasingly more disillusioned with the narrow and unimaginative education he had received at school.

▲ Tomás Garrigue Masaryk

Event: Founding the Czechoslovak nation.

Role: Tomás Garrigue Masaryk rose from poverty to become one of the intellectual and political leaders of Bohemia (which would eventually become a Czechoslovakian province) prior to World War I. During the war he led the fight for the independence of Czechoslovakia. Masaryk became the new nation's first president in late 1918.

Le Monnier asked Masaryk to serve as a tutor and companion for his son. Through the police chief's influence, Masaryk was able to enter the Akademisches Gymnasium, or Academic High School, one of Vienna's most respected high schools. He became one of the institution's best students. Eventually he passed the *abitur,* or comprehensive final exam, which allowed him to enter the University of Vienna.

Masaryk found the intellectual climate at the university too stifling for his tastes. But despite bookish and boring instruction, he managed to complete his studies in philosophy with a focus on the works of Plato. He also studied English, Russian, history, psychology, law, and logic.

Masaryk hoped to enter the diplomatic service, but he quickly learned that positions in that government agency were reserved for the sons of aristocrats. For several years he lived in poverty, supporting himself as a tutor. He graduated from the University of Vienna with a doctorate in 1876 and shortly afterwards moved to Leipzig, Germany, where he worked as a tutor for a banker.

Love and Marriage

In Leipzig, Germany, Masaryk fell in love with Charlotte Garrigue, an American who was on a tour of Europe. In 1878, after he had returned to Vienna, he learned that Charlotte had been seriously injured in a carriage accident. He set sail for New York to visit her. They married in March of that year, and Masaryk took her maiden name, Garrigue, as his middle name.

After returning to Vienna the next year, Masaryk was hired as a lecturer at the university. Later, he moved to Prague, Bohemia (later Czechoslovakia), to teach at the new Czech-language facility that had been established at Charles University, one of the oldest universities in Europe. A staunch advocate of fresh and innovative teaching techniques, Masaryk encouraged his students to ponder and analyze their subject matter. He often invited them to his home for dinner and academic discussions. While at Prague, Masaryk also found time to begin publishing *Athenaeum,* a political journal, and later to edit *Cas* (meaning "hour"), another periodical.

Czech reformer. The monarchy of Austria-Hungary spread out over two kingdoms, each of which incorporated several different languages and cultures. Masaryk had long deplored the sec-

▲ Masaryk long deplored the second-class status of Czechs and Slovaks
in the Austro-Hungarian empire. He and his colleagues demanded
reforms.

ond-class status of Czechs and Slovaks in the Austro-Hungarian
empire. He and his colleagues demanded reforms. They pushed
for the full use of the Czech language in schools and equality for
the Czech and Slovak peoples. Throughout the 1880s, Masaryk

stirred up controversy in *Athenaeum* and *Cas,* using these journals as a vehicle to attack long-held beliefs about Czech literature and history.

In Parliament. In 1891 leaders of the Young Czech Party asked Masaryk to represent them in the Austrian Parliament. While serving in both the Austrian Parliament and the Bohemian Diet, or legislative assembly, he earned a reputation as a fiery reformer. Among other things, he called for the reform of labor laws and for a federal arrangement for the Austro-Hungarian empire that would give Czechs and Slovaks some degree of self-government. He resisted party discipline, however, and soon lost interest in legislative politics. In 1895 he returned to the university.

Denouncing anti-Semitism. The following year Masaryk came to the defense of Leopold Hilsner, a Jew who was convicted of the ritual murder of two girls. At the time, Jews were mistakenly believed to murder people in order to use their blood for religious rites. Masaryk wrote a pamphlet in 1899 denouncing anti-Semitic (or anti-Jewish) superstition and condemning Hilsner's wrongful conviction and subsequent death sentence for the ludicrous charges. He suffered considerable mistreatment for defending Hilsner, especially after he decided to investigate the case himself.

A Study in Czech History

Masaryk made enemies among his fellow Czechs when he accepted an article for *Athenaeum* that questioned the authenticity of two Czech-language poems supposedly written in the Middle Ages. These poems were a source of pride to many Czechs and provided evidence of a long Czech literary history. Although the documents were later proven to be fakes, Masaryk was attacked by academics and journalists and lost the opportunity to serve as an encyclopedia editor. The controversy inspired him to undertake an intensive study of Czech history. He went on to become the leader of a group of younger Czech intellectuals who did not need forged manuscripts or exaggerations about history to boost their self-esteem.

Although Masaryk found clear evidence of Hilsner's innocence, the scholar-turned-detective was denounced and verbally abused by some Czechs and Slovaks for the next several years. Through the Hilsner case, Masaryk once again demonstrated that he had the courage to stand up for truth despite the consequences. He eventually became one of the most famous and esteemed men in Bohemia.

Turning point. Masaryk's reputation soon spread to the United States. In 1901 Charles Crane, a Chicago industrialist and friend of future U.S. president Woodrow Wilson, invited him to give a series of lectures at the University of Chicago.

The Chicago lectures were a turning point in Masaryk's career. He felt that Americans lacked the class-consciousness of Europeans and were more fearless, independent, and open-minded people. Masaryk sought to create American-style constitutional republics in Bohemia and Moravia. (He even sent his son Jan to the United States to be educated.) Masaryk's ideas turned to action when he was again elected to the Austrian Parliament in 1907. He called for the unity of Bohemia and Moravia with Slovakia, which was part of the kingdom of Hungary.

Participation: Founding the Czechoslovak Nation

Setting the stage for independence. After World War I broke out, Masaryk, still a member of Parliament, secretly began working for the independence of Bohemia, Moravia, and Slovakia. He contacted two powerful men in Great Britain—Robert Seton-Watson, a Slavonic scholar, and Henry Wickham Steed, a journalist—and secretly passed them information about conditions in Bohemia and Moravia that could be useful for the Allies (the countries siding against the Central European Powers in the war). In late 1914, while he was in Rome, Austro-Hungarian agents learned of his activities. There Masaryk received a postcard, in code, warning him that he would be arrested once he returned home. He was forced to remain in exile.

A Visit to Russia

In 1887 Masaryk visited Russia for the first time and made the acquaintance of Leo Tolstoy, the great Russian writer. The two carried on a long-running correspondence and vigorously debated various philosophical issues, including Tolstoy's pacifism (an opposition to using war or violence as a means of resisting evil or settling disputes). Masaryk came to reject this viewpoint, although he did remain friends with Tolstoy.

The Paris Manifesto. After his secret activities had been exposed, Masaryk began to campaign openly for the independence of Bohemia, Moravia, and Slovakia. He presented a series of lectures, wrote newspaper articles, and established a Czech press bureau in London. Masaryk was soon joined by Eduard Benes, a younger Czech activist who "fell completely under his spell" upon meeting him (Korbel, p. 27). Benes would eventually coin the name "Czechoslovakia" for the future republic. In November 1915 Masaryk, Benes, and other Czech nationalists issued the Paris Manifesto, declaring the revolt of the Czech nation against the Austro-Hungarian empire. Following this declaration, Czech units (composed mostly of soldiers who had defected from the Austro-Hungarian army to fight for the Allies) recognized Masaryk as their leader.

Czech fighting units. Masaryk's hopes were boosted when the Russian czar (the nation's absolute ruler) was overthrown in March 1917. He knew several members of Russia's new provisional government, which he hoped would mobilize the thousands of Czech soldiers who had defected to the Russian side. (Russia was an ally of Britain, France, and later the United States in the fight against Germany, Austria, and Turkey during World War I.) In 1917, carrying a British passport identifying him as "Thomas George Marsden," Masaryk sailed for Russia, where he attended a conference of delegates from all Czech organizations in Russia that met in Kiev. The delegates pledged themselves to support an independent Czechoslovak republic and received permission to organize a Czech army unit. Czech forces in Russia rapidly grew to seventy thousand.

> ### Defending Innocent Serbs
>
> In 1908 Masaryk defended fifty-three Serbs accused of high treason. Again demonstrating his talents as a detective, he proved that the documents used to convict them were, in fact, forged by high government officials. As a result of Masaryk's investigation, a foreign minister lost his job.

In July 1917 Czech units fought a successful rearguard (protecting the rear of withdrawing troops) action at Zborov, outperforming their Russian allies. When the Bolshevik Revolution occurred soon afterward and the Russian army began to disintegrate, only the Czech units maintained their unity.

Once the Bolsheviks—leaders of the Russian Revolution, which resulted in the formation of the Soviet Union—had made a separate peace with the Central Powers (Germany and its allies) in March 1918, the Czech forces were stranded in Russia. Their only route of escape was through the Pacific port of Vladivostok, which they would have to reach by way of the Trans-Siberian Railroad.

Joseph Stalin (see entry), the Bolshevik People's Commissar of Nationalities, gave Masaryk permission to take his troops through the vast region of Siberia, part of Asiatic Russia. From Vladivostok, they planned to sail east—all the way around the globe—to Western Europe, where they would fight on the western front. As the Czechs began to move eastward, Masaryk traveled ahead of them to Vladivostok to arrange for their transportation to Europe. He later went on to Japan and the United States. Meanwhile, fighting broke out between the Czechs and the Bolsheviks. Stalin revoked their permission to travel east through Siberia. By 1920, however, most of the Czechs reached Czechoslovakia after fighting their way to Vladivostok.

Recognition in the fight for independence. Around the same time, persistent lobbying by Benes and Slovak leader Milan Stefanik began to pay off. By the summer of 1918, the Allies had committed themselves to the liberation of Czechoslovakia. That August, the Allies recognized the Czech National Council as a legitimate ally.

In Bohemia and Moravia, sentiment for independence began to stir. Demonstrators in Prague shouted "Long live Masaryk" and unrest spread throughout the Central Powers. In July 1918 Czech politicians in Bohemia and Moravia called for a general strike, set for October, to increase pressure on the government to grant independence.

On October 14, 1918, the day of the general strike, Benes, then in exile in Paris, declared the Czech National Council a provisional government. Three days later, Masaryk issued the Washington Declaration, proclaiming the formation of the Republic of Czechoslovakia. According to the Washington Declaration, Czechoslovakia would guarantee its people freedom of

The Masaryk Family and World War I

The Masaryks endured unnerving persecution during World War I. In Prague, Masaryk's oldest daughter was arrested and imprisoned. Meanwhile, with Masaryk in exile in Italy, the police continually harassed his wife. And his son Jan, who lived in America, just happened to be vacationing in Austria when war was declared; he was forced to join the army, where he served as a cavalry officer.

speech, religion, assembly, and the press. It would provide social, cultural, and political equality for all its citizens, equality for women, and protection of the rights of ethnic minorities. In addition, the declaration called for the separation of church and state, the dissolution of large estates, and an end to aristocratic privileges.

On October 28, Czechoslovakia became independent of the crumbling Austro-Hungarian empire without a shot being fired. According to historical accounts, Masaryk learned from the shouts of newsboys in Times Square that he was the new president of Czechoslovakia. He immediately sailed for home and reached Prague on December 20, 1918.

Aftermath

Fighting communism. Czechoslovakia was in turmoil during its first years of independence. The Slovak and German minorities were uneasy, inflation was rampant, and labor unrest was widespread. In December 1920 communists organized a general strike as a means of seizing power.

Masaryk decided to fight the communists by appealing to reason. In 1920 he wrote a series of articles on communism in which he portrayed Soviet Marxism—the belief that revolution by the working class against capitalist laws would eventually lead to a classless, or socialistic, society—as tyrannical and reactionary. Masaryk stressed that social change could only come through education and evolution; the Bolsheviks, he felt, could not uproot a thousand years of tradition by violence. Masaryk pointed out that the Soviet concept of a "dictatorship of the proletariat" (working class) was "nothing else than a state of servitude" (Korbel, p. 54). As a result of his efforts, the general strike failed and labor unrest tapered off.

Anti-Bolshevik Sentiment

Masaryk disagreed with the extremist revolutionary views of Russia's Bolsheviks. He is said to have viewed Bolshevism as despotic, destructive, and reactionary and considered Bolshevik leader Vladimir Lenin a brilliant but half-educated thinker.

Efforts at reform. Masaryk pursued numerous reforms during his presidency. Large estates were broken up, and acreage restrictions were imposed on farms. He believed strongly in education, and during his administration numerous schools were built. Not all of the reforms Masaryk sought were achieved but Czechoslovakia's republican institutions began to flourish even as they withered in surrounding countries. By 1938 Czechoslovakia was surrounded by authoritarian and totalitarian regimes.

Masaryk served as president until 1935, when he resigned. Before retiring, though, he made certain that the National Assembly would accept his protégé, Eduard Benes, as his successor. Two years later, on October 14, 1937, Masaryk died.

Domination by outside forces. The republic that Masaryk fought so hard to create survived only a few more months. Shortly after the former president's death, Nazi Germany's chancellor, Adolf Hitler, threatened an invasion if Czechoslovakia did not cede the German-speaking western region of Sudetenland. Fearing a general European war, England and France agreed to Hitler's demand and pledged not to come to Czechoslovakia's defense. Although the Czechs were mobilized and ready to fight, Benes, seeing the military situation as hopeless, allowed the Nazis to occupy the Sudeten region without military retaliation. The Germans forced him to resign later in October, and by March 1939 Germany and Hungary occupied the rest of the country.

Czechoslovakia reemerged from World War II, but in February 1948 it fell under Soviet domination after the communists took power in a *coup d'etat* (a violent overthrow of an existing government). Shortly afterward, communist agents murdered Jan Masaryk, who had become Czechoslovakia's foreign minister, by throwing him from a building. Benes died soon thereafter.

For More Information

Bolton, G. *The Czech Tragedy.* London: Watts, 1955.

Korbel, Josef. *Twentieth-Century Czechoslovakia.* New York: Columbia University Press, 1977.

Zeman, Zbynek. *The Masaryks.* London: Weidenfeld & Nicholson, 1976.

Kemal Atatürk

1881-1938

Personal Background

Trained for the military. Mustafa Kemal Atatürk was born in the winter of 1881 in Thessaloniki, Macedonia, which is now a part of Greece but had been under the rule of the Ottoman Turks for five hundred years at the time of his birth. His mother raised him after his father, a customs official, died in 1888. Mustafa, as he was then known, attended a Koranic (Muslim) school, then a state high school in Thessaloniki. His mother wanted him to go to a religious school, but he wanted to pursue a military career. At the age of twelve, he entered the military secondary school in Thessaloniki. There, he was given the name Kemal, meaning "perfect." Kemal enrolled in the war college at Istanbul in 1899 and then the staff college for training as an advanced field officer. Three years later, he graduated as a general staff captain in the army of the Ottoman empire.

The Ottoman Empire was once a vast area spanning Europe, Asia, and Africa that included Turkey, Syria, Egypt, Iraq, the Barbary States, the Balkan States, Palestine, part of Arabia, and part of Russia and Hungary. The empire was nominally ruled by sultans, who over the centuries had become figurehead rulers, frequently known more for their decadence than for any kind of leadership. In reality, government officials called grand viziers ruled the Ottoman Empire. The capital of the Ottoman Empire was in

▲ Kemal Atatürk

Event: Creating the Republic of Turkey.

Role: Kemal Atatürk organized Turkish nationalist resistance against the division of Turkey at the end of World War I. Overcoming the Ottoman (or Turkish) government's passive acceptance of Allied war treaty conditions, he and his followers forced the Allied powers to agree to peace terms favorable to Turkey.

Constantinople (now Istanbul). By the time Kemal was in college, most of the empire's holdings outside of Turkey had either gained independence from the Ottoman Empire or had come under the rule of stronger European powers. In fact, the Ottoman Empire was in a severe state of decline. It had lost its economic independence and so was often at the mercy of European powers.

Antigovernment activist. While attending the war college and staff college, Kemal became active in the antigovernment activities of a growing number of Turks opposed to the oppressive regime of Sultan Abdul Hamid. Kemal read banned literature and helped to secretly publish an antigovernment newspaper. Shortly after he graduated, his activities were discovered. He was allowed to continue his military duties but was assigned to Syria, a remote location where it was hoped he would stay out of trouble. However, while serving there with a cavalry regiment, Kemal continued to spread his revolutionary ideas.

During these early years with the military Kemal became involved with the Young Turk movement, a reformist group that worked toward liberalizing the Ottoman Empire. He served a leadership role in the Young Turk revolution of 1908, which secured a constitutional government for the Ottoman Empire and deposed the sultan (although another sultan replaced him).

Defender of Istanbul. In 1914 the Ottoman empire entered World War I on the side of the Central Powers (Germany and its associates). During the subsequent fighting, Kemal established himself as a competent and heroic soldier, thereby rekindling the reputation of the long-decaying Ottoman empire.

The following year, Allied troops (which included Russia, Great Britain, France, and the United States) landed on the Gallipoli peninsula in a bid to take Istanbul (in northwestern Turkey) and capture the Bosporus and Dardanelles, the straits linking the Black Sea with the Mediterranean. A victory would have opened up a sea route to provide Russian troops with supplies. But the Allied campaign failed. Kemal ordered a division to occupy a strategic hill blocking the Allied advance, then began a series of counterattacks to drive off the enemy. When the Allies made another landing at Suvla Bay, he again succeeded in stopping the advance, despite overwhelming Allied military superiority. The Turks held their positions, and the Allies eventually withdrew from Gallipoli. For his role in saving the Ottoman capital and denying the Allies access to the Black Sea, the sultan awarded Kemal a silver medal.

Commander of Turkish troops. In 1917 Kemal accompanied the Ottoman Crown Prince Vahideddin on a visit to Germany and solidified his ties to the highest levels of the Ottoman government. He became an even stronger critic of the Central Powers' war policy.

By the next year Kemal had assumed command of troops in Syria. The soldiers had been beaten by the British in Palestine, but Kemal transformed their defeat into an orderly retreat. His troops were still fighting in Syria on October 30, when the Moudros Armistice ended the war. In addition to forcing the Ottoman empire to surrender half its territory, the agreement called for the demobilization of the army, the opening of the Bosporus and Dardanelles straits, and Allied occupation of strategic positions, such as the forts along the straits.

Participation: Creating the Republic of Turkey

Terms of surrender. The empire's troubles mounted following the armistice. Greek rebels began organizing in western Anatolia, or Asian Turkey, and Armenian rebels were organizing in the east. The Young Turk leaders who had led the empire into World War I had fled the country. The new sultan, Mehmed VI Vahideddin (whom Kemal had accompanied to Germany while he was still crown prince), hoped to stay in power by granting special favors to the Allies. He installed a pro-Allied government under Damad Ferid Pasha, whom he appointed grand vizier (the title of a high executive officer). Nevertheless, the Allies began to divide up the empire's Arab provinces, and it appeared that they would soon carve up the rest.

Using his government connections, particularly in the War Ministry and the Ministry of Posts and Telegraphs, Kemal secured an appointment as inspector of the Third Army Corps at

▲ Atatürk was determined to turn Turkey into a modern state and instituted numerous reforms based on revolutionary Western ideas.

Samsun on the Black Sea. Sympathetic government officials provided Kemal with a large staff and granted him a broad range of powers, including the authority to give orders to civilian governors. Kemal's name was on a list of so-called "unreliable officers" compiled by the British forces occupying the old empire, but they failed to arrest him.

Kemal headed for Samsun from Istanbul on a cargo boat. Shortly before he departed, Greek troops landed at Izmir,

Smyrna, near the Aegean Sea at the urging of the Western Allies. After his arrival at Samsun, Kemal immediately began to organize nationalist resistance. (Nationalists advocated complete Turkish independence and a deep sense of national pride and consciousness.) Through a telegram, he instructed provincial governors and army commanders to arrange a series of protest meetings. These meetings would provide a forum for opposition to the occupation of Izmir and for resistance to Allied intervention. Kemal also led a series of meetings himself to organize resistance.

Recall and resistance. Under the armistice, Kemal's Third Army was supposed to have been demobilized. When the British found out about Kemal's appointment and demanded his recall, the Turkish government ordered him to return to Istanbul on the first steamer. Kemal stalled, complaining about coal and gasoline shortages. By July 1919 the government finally terminated his authority, but it was too late. Kemal's power in the region was now secure. When he failed to comply with the orders from Istanbul, the government revoked his commission and decorations and declared him a rebel. The renegade Kemal then resigned from the army.

Kemal believed that Turkey's foreign policy should emphasize its national integrity and not pursue pan-Turkish (a policy of unity, stressing strictly Turkish ideas), pan-Islamic, or imperialistic policies such as the recovery of the empire's former Arab provinces. (Imperialism is the extension of a nation's power to other territories beyond its own borders.) Under his direction, the nationalist congress at Sivas in 1919 adopted the National Pact, which emphasized Turkey's political, judicial, and financial independence.

Kemal ordered army commanders loyal to the nationalists to seize telegraph facilities and called on civil authorities to respect the authority of a representative committee, or provisional government, set up by the congress. He established the nationalist headquarters in Angora (now Ankara).

Election. The sultan, whose authority was by this time confined primarily to the area around Istanbul, tried to appease Kemal by replacing his pro-Allied grand vizier, Damad Ferid Pasha, with one who agreed to hold new national elections. A vigorous election campaign by nationalist groups paid off. On January 28, 1920, the chamber approved the National Pact and asserted the independence of the Ottoman Muslim—that is, Turkish—part of the empire.

Seeking to crush the nationalists, the Allies occupied Istanbul in March, arrested several nationalist legislators and more than 150 intellectuals, and deported them to Malta. The sultan then reappointed Damad Ferid Pasha as grand vizier. Damad promptly ordered the breakup of the Chamber of Deputies. He then persuaded the sultan, in his capacity as head of the Muslim religion, to issue a *fatwa,* or decree, ordering the killing of all nationalist rebels as a religious duty. In response, Kemal had a religious council in Angora issue a *fatwa* that accused the sultan of betraying his country to the Allies.

A Call for a Turkish Nation

In Erzurum, in eastern Anatolia, Kemal convened a conference of nationalists in a classroom at an Armenian school. Under his leadership, the delegates voted to resist further attempts by the Greeks to occupy Anatolia. In September 1919 nationalists held another meeting—this one at Sivas in central Anatolia. Under Kemal's leadership, delegates called for the election of a national assembly capable of organizing a strong government and concluding a satisfactory peace settlement.

Shaping a government. Far from crushing the nationalists, the Allied occupation of Istanbul only inflamed them. In April 1920 Kemal ordered the deputies who had been expelled from Istanbul to meet in Angora to convene what would later be known as the Grand National Assembly. The members voted to retain the 1876 Ottoman constitution. Although Kemal wanted to proclaim a republic, he faced considerable opposition on this issue and was forced to yield to the delegates' desire to retain the sultan.

Objecting to the peace terms. Nationalist sentiments were further stirred when Greek premier Eleutherios Venizelos revealed the Treaty of Sevres in May 1920. The pact called for Greece to acquire Izmir and eastern Thrace (a northeast region of Greece; Thrace is divided between Turkey, Greece, and Bulgaria), demanded the creation of an independent Armenia and Kurdistan, and stipulated that an international administration of the straits be formed and run by the Allies. In addition, the Allies would continue to supervise the Turkish government, and the British, French, and Italians would establish spheres of influence in Anatolia, giving them exclusive commercial rights. The sultan's government signed the treaty, although it would have virtually terminated Turkey's independence had its provisions been carried out.

The next month, Greece began a full-scale invasion of Anatolia (the Asian Ottoman empire). With 150,000 Greek troops in Anatolia, the nationalists appeared to be facing formidable odds. In addition, Great Britain, France, and Italy had troops in Anatolia, and Armenian guerrillas were organized for active fighting. However, the Allied powers, who were rapidly demobilizing following World War I, had no desire to wage a full-scale war in Turkey. And the French began to see the advantage of a friendly Turkish government to the north of Syria and Lebanon, where they were fighting to establish colonial rule. Along with the Italians, they soon withdrew from Anatolia and even began selling arms to the nationalists. In England, sentiment grew in favor of a strong Turkey as a defensive wall against the spread of communism to the Balkans and Middle East.

After the pro-Allied Greek king died from the infectious bite of a pet monkey, his subjects chose as his replacement a king who had favored the Central Powers. The Allies then withdrew their support for

Commander in Chief

In the midst of the war with Greece, Kemal convinced the Grand National Assembly to appoint him commander in chief, a title previously held only by the sultan. In July 1922 this title was made permanent.

Greece. But the Greeks persisted and fought their way to the Sakarya River, about fifty miles from Angora. Greek and Turkish soldiers fought a three-week-long battle there that cost each side about twenty thousand lives. Although the Greeks declared victory, they had been forced to halt their advance.

The Greeks then tried to negotiate an agreement for withdrawal, but Kemal insisted on an unconditional removal of Greek troops. On August 26, 1922, Turkish forces penetrated the Greek lines and defeated the Greek army. After taking Izmir, the Turks burned the city and killed thousands of its Greek inhabitants.

New treaty. In 1923, after the fighting had ceased, Kemal's government concluded the Treaty of Lausanne with the Allied powers. The pact recognized Kemal's success on the battlefield, gave Turkey control of eastern Thrace, and called for Greeks liv-

▲ Atatürk reviewing his troops; in the midst of the war with Greece, Kemal convinced the Grand National Assembly to appoint him commander in chief.

ing in Turkey to return to Greece and Turks living in Greece to return to Turkey. However, the Turks were not permitted to occupy the straits until 1935, when they eventually won the right to do so at the Montreux Convention.

Reform. Having gained full control of Turkey, Kemal began to do away with the last vestiges of the dying Ottoman empire. He abolished the sultanate in 1923 and proclaimed Turkey a republic, which would be headed by a powerful president elected by the legislature. As Turkey's first president, Kemal ruled as a virtual dictator, ruthlessly suppressing all opposition.

Building a modern nation. Kemal was determined to turn Turkey into a modern state and instituted numerous reforms based on revolutionary Western ideas. In 1924 he abolished the traditional civil and religious courts and ordered numerous Islamic orders, brotherhoods, and sects dissolved. In 1925 he passed the "hat law," which prohibited the wearing of the *fez,* a brimless hat worn by devout Muslims, and decreed the wearing of European-style hats. Other reforms included the outlawing of polygamy and some forms of divorce, the adoption of the Gregorian calendar, and the use of the Latin alphabet. (An Arabic script had long been used as the written form of the Turkish language.) Kemal also ruled that all Turks must take a surname. In 1935 the national assembly gave him the name Atatürk, which means "Chief Turk" or "Father of the Turks."

In foreign policy, Kemal took paths he felt would make Turkey a modern part of the community of nations. In 1930 he concluded a peace treaty with Greece, ending a century of conflict with this Balkan neighbor. He also remained on friendly terms with the Soviet Union and other states in the region. In 1932 Turkey joined the League of Nations.

Death of Atatürk. In January 1938 Kemal was diagnosed with cirrhosis of the liver, probably the result of a lifetime of heavy drinking. His health deteriorated rapidly. On November 10, while still holding office, he died after falling into a coma. The Republic of Turkey, which he founded, continues to endure.

For More Information

Churchill, Winston S. *The Aftermath (The World Crisis, 1918-1929).* New York: Charles Scribner's Sons, 1929.

Kuniholm, Bruce R. *The Origins of the Cold War in the Near East.* Princeton, New Jersey: Princeton University Press, 1980.

Macfie, A. L. *Atatürk.* London: Longmans, 1994.

Rustow, Dankwart A. "The Army and the Founding of the Turkish Republic." *World Politics,* July 1959, pp. 513-52.

Joseph Stalin

1879-1953

Personal Background

Born in Georgia. Joseph Stalin was born Iosif Vissari-onovich Dzhugashvili on December 21, 1879, in Gori, Georgia—a part of czarist Russia's empire in western Asia. (One ruler, called a czar in Russia, exercised unlimited power over the people.) His father, a former serf, was a shoemaker, and his mother was a domestic servant.

Iosif, or Joseph, better known as "Soso," grew up speaking Georgian and only learned Russian at the age of eight or nine. In 1888 he began attending the church school at Gori. He did well in his classes, especially in religious studies, geography, and Georgian. He also studied Greek and Russian. When he left the school in 1894, he was near the top of his class.

Stalin's mother wanted him to become a priest and was disappointed when he pursued another course in life. Years later, even after he had become leader of the Soviet Union, she considered him a failure for not having completed his religious studies.

Seminary student. Stalin won a scholarship to study at the Tbilisi Theological Seminary, Georgia's leading educational institution. During his first year there, he received high marks; the next year, however, he began to rebel against the institution's stern religious rules. He smuggled banned books into school, and

▲ **Joseph Stalin**

Event: Building the Union of Soviet Socialist Republics.

Role: Joseph Stalin took control of the Soviet Union after the death of Bolshevik party leader Vladimir Lenin. During his dictatorial rule of the Soviet state, Stalin launched an ambitious program to develop heavy industry and collective (or communal, state-controlled) agriculture.

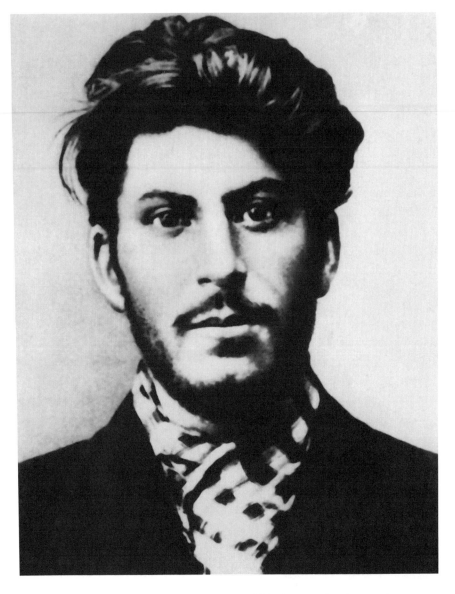

▲ A young Stalin; in 1899 Stalin obtained his first and only regular employment outside of the Communist Party organization when he was hired as an accountant. After he was fired he became a professional revolutionary.

at one point he was sent to a punishment cell for five hours for not bowing to a school official. By 1899 the seminary directors could stand no more of his antics. He was expelled.

Discovery of Marx. In about 1896 or 1897, while still at the seminary, Stalin began reading Marxist works, focusing especially on the writings of Russian Marxist Vladimir Lenin. Marxism—the belief that a revolution by the working class would eventually lead to a classless society—would furnish the basis of Stalin's worldview for the rest of his life. Stalin seems to have thought of himself as a champion of the people. He began using the pseudonym "Koba," after a fictional hero in Georgian literature whom he admired.

In 1899 Stalin obtained his first and only regular employment outside of the Communist Party organization when he was hired as an accountant at the Tbilisi observatory. (Communism is a political system based on communal ownership of all property.) Russia's Social Democrats, members of a Communist Party opposed by the czar, had been using the observatory as a hideout, and Stalin ultimately joined them. A police raid exposed this association, and he was fired from his accounting job. From this point on, Stalin was a professional revolutionary.

Early days as a revolutionary. At the turn of the twentieth century, Stalin became active in the militant wing of the Russian Social Democratic Party. He was arrested in 1902 and deported to Siberia, but he escaped and was back in Georgia two years later. He first met Lenin, leader of the Bolshevik faction of the Social Democratic Party, in 1905 and became a devoted follower. Lenin secretly approved of bank robberies, which he called "expropriations," to finance the Bolsheviks. In 1907 Stalin was involved in several bank heists in Georgia. To avoid connection with any illegal activities, the local party expelled him, and he disappeared.

Stalin soon reappeared in Baku in Azerbaijan (a region of the former Soviet Union near the Caspian Sea), where he began organizing a Bolshevik faction. He spent the next few years in and out of trouble, spending time in exile in Siberia for his revolutionary activities.

Associated with Lenin. In 1912 Lenin broke from the Social Democratic Party and formed a new party. Seeing Stalin as a "ruthless and dependable enforcer of the Bolsheviks' will" (Conquest, p. 48), Lenin nominated him to the party's Central Committee. However, Stalin was arrested shortly thereafter and exiled once again to Siberia, where he remained until the czar was overthrown in 1917.

Participation: Building the Union of Soviet Socialist Republics

The new Soviet government. After the overthrow of the czar in the Russian Revolution, the Bolsheviks took over the Russian government in 1917. Lenin, the new ruler of Russia, named Stalin to his cabinet as Commissar of Nationalities. In this capacity, Stalin planted Bolshevik officials among the various ethnic groups in Russia in an effort to bring them under Moscow's rule. He also used his position to influence Bolshevik leaders such as Vyachislav Molotov, Lazar Kaganovich, and Dmitri Voroshilov, who would support him in his drive for power.

Becoming "Stalin"

By 1917 Joseph Dzhugashvili, who had used several pseudonyms, was calling himself "Stalin," which comes from the Russian word *stal'*, meaning "steel." This could have been a Russification of Dzhugashvili, as *dzhuga* means "iron" in a Georgian dialect.

Lenin came to admire Stalin for his loyalty and dedication. Stalin appeared to enjoy the tediousness of office work, but he could also be a fierce and decisive leader. In 1920 American communist John Reed observed: "[Stalin's] not an intellectual.... He's not even well informed, but he knows what he wants. He's got the will-power, and he's going to be at the top of the pile some day" (Conquest, p. 96).

Beginning in 1919, Lenin set up a number of agencies to manage government affairs. A zealous supporter of the communist cause, Stalin volunteered to be a member of various party committees and newly formed agencies. The most important of these new agencies was the Secretariat, which grew from thirty members in 1919 to more than six hundred in 1922. That year, Lenin gave Stalin "formal possession of [the] private little empire" he had so lovingly assembled by making him general secretary of the party Central Committee (Johnson, p. 84).

Taking control. Under Stalin, the Secretariat became the Communist Party's real center of power. As general secretary, he had the power to appoint local secretaries who would, in turn,

▲ Vladimir Lenin and Stalin in 1922; seeing Stalin as a "ruthless and dependable enforcer of the Bolsheviks' will," Lenin nominated him to the party's Central Committee.

select delegates to party congresses. In this manner, Stalin gradually packed the party's legislative bodies and staff with his own supporters.

In May 1922 Lenin suffered the first of a series of debilitating strokes, and his health began to deteriorate. Later that year, he expressed second thoughts about having given Stalin so much power. He dictated a document known as his "testament," which severely criticized Stalin, although it also contained criticism of the other leading Bolsheviks. As Lenin's illness worsened, though, he lost virtually all of his influence. Lenin was faulted by the Bolsheviks for allegedly compromising on some of the Com-

29

munist Party's ideals, and political turmoil began to brew in the Soviet Union even before his death in January 1924.

After Lenin died, the party, now called the All-Union Communist Party, was headed by a "collective leadership" that included Stalin; Leon Trotsky, who had organized the Red Army (the official name of the Soviet Army) and still headed it; Lev Kamenev and Grigori Zinoviev, the party bosses in Moscow and Leningrad, respectively; and Nikolai Bukharin, the party's leading theorist. Each of these men was ambitious and hoped to serve as the party's next leader.

A shrewd and ruthless politician, Stalin was able to maneuver his opponents out of power by skillfully manipulating their jealousies and personal rivalries. First, he aligned himself with Kamenev and Zinoviev against Trotsky, who was soon ousted as head of the army. (He was driven into exile in 1929 and killed by one of Stalin's agents in Mexico City.)

Next, Stalin teamed up with Bukharin in order to move against Kamenev and Zinoviev. He defended the New Economic Policy (NEP), a series of free-market reforms introduced by Lenin in 1921 that were supported by Bukharin. Stalin also endorsed Bukharin's proposal that the Soviets should build "socialism in one country" rather than waste their efforts on trying to incite world revolution. Meanwhile, Stalin's agents within the party undermined popular support for Kamenev and Zinoviev. Delegates at the Fourteenth Party Congress in 1925 voted to expel them both.

Stalin then turned against Bukharin, who met secretly with Kamenev and Zinoviev, warning that Stalin would eventually "strangle" them if not stopped (Johnson, p. 266). However, it was by this time much too late: Stalin had gained absolute control of the party and by 1927 he was well established as dictator of the Soviet Union. He later had Kamenev, Zinoviev, and Bukharin shot.

Leader of the Soviet Union. Once in control of the Soviet Union, Stalin began to push a plan for rapid, forced industrialization and the collectivization of agriculture. The organization of farming around small family farms, Stalin believed, produced uncontrollable "anarchic" and "capitalist" forces. (Anarchy is a state of disorder

▲ Stalin believed that the Soviet Union had to undergo a transformation into a great industrial power if it were to be taken seriously as a "great world power."

resulting from a lack of government authority; capitalism is an economic system based on private ownership and free market ideals.) Stalin decided to push for full and immediate action on a plan that would force farmers to abandon their individual farms and move onto state-owned "collective" farms (Malia, p. 222).

Although the Soviet economy was in a shambles and food in the cities was in short supply, collectivization and forced industrialization would fulfill a number of needs. For one thing, the change would rapidly add to Stalin's "proletarian" (industrial worker) base in a party that ruled a largely agricultural country. Many Marxists were by this time tired of compromising with capitalism; they longed for a "socialist offensive" that would hasten the pace of change. Stalin also believed that the Soviet Union had to undergo a transformation into a great industrial power if it were to be taken seriously as a "great world power."

The Five-Year Plan. Stalin's "Five-Year Plan" for industrialization officially began in 1928. Factories, dams, and other enterprises were constructed all across the Soviet Union in accordance with grandiose plans drawn up by government planning agencies. In late 1932 the plan was declared a success. Soviet factories were by then producing basic industrial products such as steel, machine tools, and tractors.

However, these achievements had a high cost and caused much suffering for the Russian people. Workers were paid low wages, and many made only enough to buy the basic necessities of life and little else. Consumer goods and food were often scarce. Changing jobs without permission became illegal, and interior passports were issued to restrict free movement among citizens. Much of the construction work on canals, mines, and other enterprises was performed by political prisoners who were sent by the millions into the Gulag, a network of labor camps for people accused of committing crimes against the state. Anyone accused of sabotage (deliberate destructive acts by a discontented employee against an employer) or "wrecking" could be shot. Beginning in 1928, "show trials" of saboteurs were staged as a warning to dissidents and as a means of instilling fear among the populace of "foreign agents."

Meanwhile, in late 1929 the government moved to collectivize agriculture, but this policy met with massive resistance from the farmers, who resented being driven from their land. Those who resisted were labeled *kulaks* (meaning "tightwads") and were characterized as greedy, wealthy farmers who exploited their poorer neighbors. The government ruthlessly pursued its drive to collectivize the rural population. Millions of kulaks were shot or sent to labor camps. In the Ukraine, South Russia, and Khazakstan, millions more died in artificial famines created when Soviet officials confiscated the farmers' grain. By 1939 most of Soviet agriculture had been collectivized.

Because of the ensuing chaos, Stalin eased up somewhat on his collectivization policy. Collective farmers were then allowed to keep their own houses and tools and to grow food for their own use in small, private gardens. Some experts claim, however, that Soviet agriculture has never recovered from the damage done by the collectivization policy begun by Stalin.

Building his image. Although Stalin had stayed in the background during the years of the Soviet Union's power struggle, he developed a so-called "cult of personality" around himself. Dozens of cities, towns, and villages were named after him, as was the tallest mountain in the Soviet Union. His name was even mentioned in the Soviet national anthem.

Stalin's obsessions. Despite all this slavish admiration and his near-total power, Stalin maintained an irrational fear of his enemies. In December 1934 Sergei Kirov, one of his old supporters, was murdered. The evidence of Stalin's involvement in the murder is strong, but it has never been proven. Still, Kirov's popularity among some Communist Party leaders may have angered Stalin. However, Stalin blamed the murder on his old enemies Kamenev and Zinoviev and then launched a series of purges (a method of removing or eliminating unwanted elements or members from an organization) in which millions of people were eventually shot or sent to the Gulag. Stalin personally signed orders for the execution of thousands of Soviet citizens.

> ## The Results of Collectivism
>
> In the midst of World War II, Stalin reportedly told British prime minister Winston Churchill that the collectivization of Russian farms—which forced 26,000,000 farmers onto 250,000 collective farms and spawned devastating "artificial" famines—had cost the lives of 10,000,000 Soviet people. (Spielvogel, p. 960)

In a move that seriously impaired the Soviet Union's ability to defend itself, Stalin ordered a purge of the armed forces in 1937 that took the lives of most of the country's marshals, generals, and admirals. When World War II broke out a few years later, the Soviet Union would suffer severely for its lack of trained military leaders.

By 1939 the Soviet Union's industrial base had been established and the nation's agriculture collectivized. Stalin slowed down the pace of the purges, although by 1940 there were fifteen million people in the Gulag. That year, Stalin's government made an agreement with Nazi leader Adolf Hitler of Germany to divide Eastern Europe between them—an agreement that freed Hitler of concern over his eastern frontier and helped to set off World War II.

Aftermath

Germany violates its agreement. Germany invaded the Soviet Union in 1941, forcing it into World War II on the side of the Allies (which included Great Britain, France, and the United States). When the war ended in 1945, the Soviets demanded and received control over much of Eastern Europe.

"Cold War" history. Stalin began another series of purges after the war and reinstituted repressive measures that had been eased during the war. He then launched a so-called "Cold War" of propaganda, subversion, and threats against the Western Allies. As he grew older, his fears and suspicions increased, and eventually he trusted no one. On March 5, 1953, as he was apparently preparing another round of purges, he died of internal bleeding following a stroke.

Stalin's economic planning and collective farms characterized the economy of the Soviet Union throughout the rest of the twentieth century. But he is perhaps most vividly remembered for his horrible legacy of death. During his rule, Stalin is estimated by some to have been responsible for the deaths of about twenty million people.

How One Collective Farm Worked

"When the harvest was over, and after the farm had met its obligations to the state and to various special funds (for insurance, seed, etc.) and had sold on the market whatever undesignated produce was left, the remaining produce and the farm's monetary income were divided among the kolkholz [collective] members according to the number of "labor days" each one had contributed to the farm's work.... After they had received their earnings at the rate of 1 kilogram of grain and 55 kopecks per labor day, one of them remarked, 'You will live, but you will be very, very thin.'" (Max Belov, *The History of a Collective Farm*, quoted in Spielvogel, p. 961)

For More Information

Conquest, Robert. *Stalin: Breaker of Nations.* New York: Viking Penguin, 1991.
Johnson, Paul. *Modern Times.* New York: St. Martin's, 1983.

Malia, Martin. *The Soviet Tragedy: A History of Socialism in Russia, 1917-1991.* New York: Free Press, 1994.

Spielvogel, Jackson J. *Western Civilization.* 2nd ed. St. Paul, Minnesota: West, 1994.

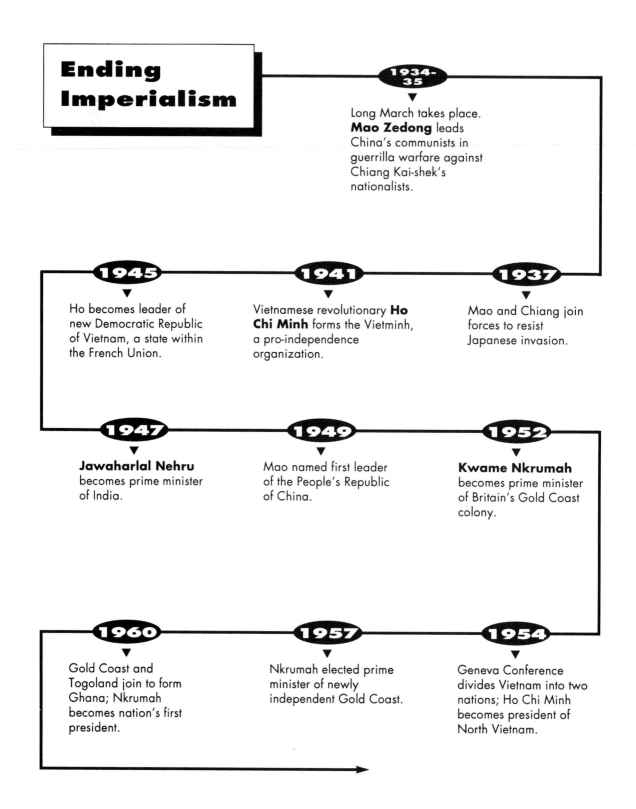

Ending Imperialism

1934-35
Long March takes place. **Mao Zedong** leads China's communists in guerrilla warfare against Chiang Kai-shek's nationalists.

1937
Mao and Chiang join forces to resist Japanese invasion.

1941
Vietnamese revolutionary **Ho Chi Minh** forms the Vietminh, a pro-independence organization.

1945
Ho becomes leader of new Democratic Republic of Vietnam, a state within the French Union.

1947
Jawaharlal Nehru becomes prime minister of India.

1949
Mao named first leader of the People's Republic of China.

1952
Kwame Nkrumah becomes prime minister of Britain's Gold Coast colony.

1954
Geneva Conference divides Vietnam into two nations; Ho Chi Minh becomes president of North Vietnam.

1957
Nkrumah elected prime minister of newly independent Gold Coast.

1960
Gold Coast and Togoland join to form Ghana; Nkrumah becomes nation's first president.

ENDING IMPERIALISM

After World War I the territories in Asia and Africa that had been dominated by European nations began to clamor for independence. The era of imperialism—the extension of a nation's power beyond its own borders—was coming to an end. France held vast areas in southeast Asia; Great Britain and Germany had extended their influence over China, and Japan was looking toward that nation for expansion; and Britain had for decades ruled over states in the Indian subcontinent, uniting some of them into a British-governed India.

By the late nineteenth century most of the large European states were moving to divide the whole of Africa. The British had found gold in southwestern Africa and established a colony there called the Gold Coast. But around the 1920s, as its territories became less and less productive, the British government began to think of giving self-rule to India and parts of Africa. Meanwhile, between the world wars, France restructured its holdings in southeast Asia. In the process, Vietnam came to be treated independently, separated from Laos, Cambodia, and other areas of French Indo-China.

The postwar push for independence. World War II took its toll on all of Europe. After the war, the people of the colonies pushed for independence. Britain was prepared to abandon its imperial claims, France was grudgingly ready to make concessions in Asia, and a newcomer to imperialism, Japan, was forced to yield its claims to places like Korea and the coast of China.

India. Local leaders rose in Asia and Africa to organize the movement for independence. In India, **Jawaharlal Nehru** made early demands for independence. Joined by Indian nationalist leader Mohandas Gandhi, he succeeded in persuading the British to proceed with plans to make India a separate nation within the British Commonwealth. Both Gandhi and Nehru saw the formation of a free India in 1947. Gandhi was assassinated the next year, but Nehru served for seventeen years as the first prime minister of the new India.

The case of China. Meanwhile, China experienced an anti-foreign rebellion called the Boxer Rising. The movement was a violent response to the intrusion of European nations. China had endured its own civil war and the overthrow of the old Manchu government early in the century. In addition, it had fought hard to resist a Japanese invasion as World War I started—and then watched in horror as German holdings along the China coast were transferred to Japan (China's nearest and most feared enemy) in post-World War I agreements.

Meanwhile, Chinese leaders like Sun Yat-sen and Chiang Kai-shek (also spelled Jiang Jieshi) sought to restore a stable government in China. Some leaders turned toward Russia for help and discovered communism, a political system based on the elimination of private property. Dominated by the doctrine of the new Soviet leaders, **Mao Zedong** (also spelled Mao Tse-tung) adopted communism, wrested control of China from the nationalists of Chiang Kai-shek and created a new government with a Soviet-style name: the People's Republic of China. Even though Mao later distanced himself from some of the Soviets' ideas, his Chinese communist government often converted citizens to the new ideology by force. Chairman Mao, as he came to be called, dominated China until 1976.

Vietnam and the Gold Coast. Ho Chi Minh also looked toward the Soviet Union and accepted communism as the best possible replacement for imperialism. In the 1940s he declared an independent Vietnam, but his pronouncement was a bit premature. Ho proceeded to lead a fight first against the French and then against the United States. The conflict continued for nearly two decades until the United States withdrew from Vietnam in 1973, four years after his death.

Three years after India and Pakistan gained independence, and just as the prolonged battle for southeast Asia was beginning, Britain decided to divest itself of another imperial colony, this one in Africa. Britain had declared the West African region of the Gold Coast as one of its crown colonies. In addition, it claimed Togoland as a protectorate, or dependent state. While still under British rule, a portion of Togoland was combined with the crown colony into a single nation called the Gold Coast. Free elections were announced and the socialist Convention People's Party emerged as the national power. In 1957 that party's candidate, **Kwame Nkrumah,** became the first prime minister of the Gold Coast. As the remaining part of British Togoland elected to join the Gold Coast, Nkrumah took charge of a new nation. He became head of state in 1960, when the Gold Coast achieved full independence from Britain as Ghana. Nkrumah was committed to developing a uniquely African form of socialism.

The Philippines. The United States was also prepared to give up its imperialist ideas. Before World War II began, plans were being formed to give independence to the Philippines. As the war ended, plans for a free Philippines resumed. The island nation became independent of the United States on July 4, 1946, with Manuel Roxas as its first president. Although U.S. interests would continue to dominate Philippine politics for many years, the period from 1930 to 1950 marks the official end of Western imperialism.

Mao Zedong

1893-1976

Personal Background

Farmer. Mao Zedong (Mao Tse-tung) was born December 26, 1893, in Shaoshan, a small farming village in China's south-central Hunan province. His father, Mao Jen-sheng, had been born in poverty and entered the imperial army as a young man. He saved money from his army pay and bought a small farm for the family.

Mao Zedong's mother, Wen Chi-mei, was a Buddhist and thus opposed to killing any living thing. Mao would later remember her loving care and her most important advice: "You should strive to be good" (Marrin, p. 7). But historians characterize Mao's father as a bitter, explosive, and miserly man. Mao began working for him on the family farm at the age of six and was forced to take on the most horrible tasks: hauling human and animal waste two buckets at a time to the rice fields. Mao Zedong was once quoted as saying, "My father was bad" (Marrin, p. 7).

Education. Mao Jen-sheng's thriftiness provided enough money for his oldest son's education. At the age of eight, Mao Zedong began formal training in the village school. The school was Confucian, teaching the ancient doctrine of Confucius, the Chinese philosopher who stressed the importance of harmonious organization—everyone knowing his or her place in society and remaining in it.

▲ **Mao Zedong**

Event: Founding the People's Republic of China.

Role: Mao Zedong joined the Communist Party in China as a young man and openly advocated violent rebellion as a way to overthrow the declining Manchu government. Following the Chinese civil war, which pitted the communists against the nationalists, the victorious Mao, now a powerful leader of the communists, proclaimed the formation of the People's Republic of China.

Mao was an excellent student and an avid reader, but the poor were denied access to the best educational institutions. Farm boys were not allowed to attend the University of Beijing. However, Mao was able to enroll in the teacher training school at Changsha, the capital of the Hunan province.

All around him, Mao saw evidence that China was collapsing. For thousands of years, the country had been controlled by dynasties, powerful ruling families that held control of provinces or regions of China for long periods of time—sometimes for centuries. In the the Manchu or Ch'ing dynasty that ruled during Mao's youth, foreigners invaded China, sparking civil wars. Chinese peasants suffered. Sun Yat-sen, a founding member of China's Nationalist Party, led a revolution in 1912 in which the Manchus were overthrown and a new government was formed. However, Sun could not unify the country and by 1916 power had fallen into the hands of military generals, or warlords, who controlled the numerous provinces in the country.

The Words of Mao Zedong

"It is man's social being that determines his thinking. Once the correct ideas characteristic of the advanced class are grasped by the masses, these ideas turn into a material force which changes society and changes the world." (Mao Tse-tung, p. 206)

Mao was exposed to Western thought at the training school. During his time there, he met a dynamic teacher, Yang Ch'ang-chi, who had lost faith in the dictatorial Chinese government. Yang's lessons had a profound influence on his student. Mao himself had witnessed the Boxer Rising (an anti-foreign rebellion in China at the turn of the twentieth century) and the overthrow of the Manchu empire in. He had observed the inherent weakness of the new Chinese government and began writing articles that criticized government policies.

Beijing and rebellion. Though Mao could not be admitted to the University of Beijing, he was allowed to work there. After graduating from the teachers' school, he moved to Beijing (Peking) and took a job as a university library assistant. Around the same time, in 1919, the Conference of Versailles completed the terms for ending World War I. Germany had long held some seaports on the Chinese mainland, a condition that China condoned for the sake of trade. The Versailles conference awarded these ports to Japan, a longtime enemy and threat to China. Students and teachers throughout China protested this arrangement, and talk at the university increased about changing the weak government.

Turn toward Russia. Feeling betrayed by the Western allies (which included Great Britain, France, and the United States) because of their postwar gift to Japan, the Chinese began to look for political models in other areas of the world. Russia had just put an end to the long rule of the czars (Russian rulers with absolute authority) and entered into a period of socialist reorganization. (Socialism is a political theory in which the government distributes goods and controls the means of production.) No translations of the writings of Karl Marx, the father of communist socialism, existed in China, but observers there watched Russia carefully. On May 4, 1919, a group of students at the University of Beijing met and decided to form a political party. Their activities soon led to the revolutionary demonstration called the May Fourth Movement, which then spread throughout the country. Two years later, the Chinese Communist Party was officially formed. Mao Zedong was among the organizers.

> ## The Family of Mao
>
> Mao Zedong married his first wife, Yang Kai-hui of Peking, in 1920. The couple had two sons, Mao An-ying and Mao An-qing. When they were still quite young, the sons were shipped off to Russia for training. Around 1928 Mao fell in love with another woman, Ho Tzu-chen, and made her his wife. He then divorced Ho to marry an actress named Jiang Qing ("Green River"). Jiang Qing was never respected by the Communist Central Committee. After Mao's death she tried with three others to take control of China. She was later arrested but refused to confess her involvement in the plot. In court she snarled, "I was Chairman Mao's dog. Whoever he told me to bite, I bit" (Marrin, p. 268).

An attempt to stabilize the Chinese government. In Canton, a city in south China, a new government was taking shape. Sun Yat-sen, a founding member of China's Nationalist Party, had been educated in the West and returned home to try to form a government that would unite his native land. Seeking to fight corruption within the Chinese government and quash the growing threat of Japanese invasion, he sought assistance from nations in the West—but received no help. Sun then turned to the newly formed Soviet Union (U.S.S.R.) for aid.

Meanwhile, conditions were worsening in Beijing. Britain held firmly to its trade arrangements there and supported Japan's

▲ Chiang Kai-shek; the nationalist-communist struggle was long and bitter; Chiang led a powerful nationalist army against Mao's smaller group of communist guerrilla fighters.

rights in China. On May 30, 1925, several students were killed during a clash at the university. Britain and Japan were implicated in the incident, causing even more antagonism toward foreign interests in China. In such an environment of political and social turmoil, the Communist Party came to be viewed as an alternative to both weak government and the influence of the West.

Participation:
Founding the People's Republic of China

The nationalists and Chiang Kai-shek. By 1927 there were two political organizations fighting over the right to unify China. Chiang Kai-shek (also spelled Jiang Jieshi) had taken over the nationalist organization (the Koumintang) of Sun Yat-sen, while Mao Zedong became a leader of the Communist Party. The nationalists wanted to keep control of China in the hands of landowners and businessmen, but the communists wanted the country turned over to the peasantry. In April 1927, fearing the influence of the communists, Chiang turned his army against them, slaughtering thousands. During the next seven years, Mao and other communists hid in remote mountainous regions in southern China. They successfully built a strong rebel government in this area, attracting more and more people to the cause. The nationalist-communist struggle was long and bitter; Chiang led a powerful army against Mao's smaller group of guerrilla fighters.

> ### Mao's Influence
>
> Mao was an impressive figure, more than six feet tall, slender and muscular, with brilliant black hair. His stature commanded respect, but no more than his intellect. Mao's words became known and respected throughout China. He wrote two books that would become guides for the Chinese communists: *Strategic Problems in the Anti-Japanese Guerrilla War* and *On Protracted War.*

The battle for authority within China continued even as the Japanese threatened to take over the entire country in the early 1930s. Fighting between the followers of Chiang and Mao continued. In 1934-35 about one hundred thousand communists under Mao began a 6,000-mile journey to the north that is now known as the Long March. During the march, the Communists fought battles and suffered incredible hardships. By the time they reached their destination the following year, more than half the original marchers had died. Mao then regrouped his communist forces in the far northwest province of Shensi. From his new base of operations, Mao Zedong set himself up to become chairman of the Chi-

45

nese Communist Party—leader of all communists in China. The communist government then declared its own war on Japan.

Two years later Japan declared war on China as the rest of the world edged toward World War II. In 1937 the threat from Japan temporarily united the nationalist-communist forces in a common struggle to save the Chinese nation.

War with Japan. The large force of Chinese nationalists battled hard against the Japanese. Chiang and his followers, the Koumintang, fought for city after city waiting for a world war to erupt that would draw Western interest to the plight of China. But the war with the Japanese would press on for seven years.

Mao and the communists. Mao's speeches and writings were designed to draw the average Chinese citizen to the communist cause. Mao felt that the success of his style of warfare, which consisted of guerrilla-type raids, depended largely on the cooperation of the Chinese people. His forces fought in front of the Japanese, at their backs, and in ambushes on all sides. In response, Japanese General Okamura devised a new war plan called *Sanko Seisako* ("The Three Alls"): "Kill all, burn all, loot all." Mao answered with an unyielding slogan of his own: "When he burns, we put out the fire. When he loots, we attack. When he pursues, we hide. When he retreats, we return" (Mao in Marrin, p. 144).

The cost of Japanese invasion. Still, the Japanese were successful. One million soldiers trained in the Japanese tradition of *bushido* (meaning "the way of the warrior") were sent to northern China to fight Mao's forces. Between 1941 and 1943, twenty-five million Chinese were killed or taken as slaves by the Japanese. Yet in the midst of their resistance to these tortures, Chiang and Mao remained enemies.

The cruelty of the Koumintang and the Japanese helped Mao win many more Chinese to communism. Between the start of fighting in 1937 and its end in 1945, Mao's Eighth Route Army swelled with peasant volunteers from 50,000 to 950,000.

The real enemy. When World War II ended in 1945, Japan agreed to return all occupied Chinese territories to the Chinese government. At the time, Allied forces recognized Chiang Kai-

▲ Chairman Mao, as he came to be called, dominated China until 1976.

shek's Koumintang as the official government. Mao was outraged. Under pressure from the United States, Mao and Chiang finally signed a meaningless pledge of a mutual desire for peace and unity. Chiang then invited Mao to attend an opera performance. During this performance, Mao's car was shot at and his driver was killed. At an after-dinner banquet, Mao made a sarcastic toast to the "long life" of Chiang Kai-shek (Marrin, p. 161). The next day he returned to Yenan, the headquarters of the Chinese Communist Party, and began preparing for the "War of Liberation."

The War of Liberation. The year 1945 marked the beginning of a Cold War between the Western allies and the Soviet Union. (A cold war is a state of heightened tension between two nations without actual military confrontation.) Soviet-style communism seemed oppressive and in direct opposition to the Western ideals of individual freedom, so the United States became uneasy and concerned over the prospect of Mao's brand of communism taking hold in China. Chiang's army, which already outnumbered the communists four to one, was armed with U.S. weapons—tanks, planes, and warships. Still, the spirit of the Koumintang was weak.

China had been virtually destroyed by the Japanese. Mao used anti-American sentiment to convert more peasants to communism. Then, in 1947, Chiang decided to attack the communist headquarters at Yenan with a massive air strike. Mao had learned of the plan in advance and ordered the city evacuated.

The War of Liberation had begun. From his retreat, Mao attacked, sweeping through the countryside and drawing the peasants to his side. By October 1948 many of the large cities were in communist hands, and Chiang had lost three hundred thousand soldiers. The Koumintang began a reign of terror to try to persuade the Chinese peasants to resist communism. At the end of 1948 the Red (Communist) Army had grown so that it outnumbered Chiang's forces. Mao by now was a brilliant military strategist. He directed his armies south and east from Manchuria, capturing city after city and easily taking the capital at Beijing. In the fall of 1949 Chiang's army was cornered in the south and preparing to escape to the island of Taiwan. On October 1, Chairman Mao declared the unification of the People's Republic of China.

Aftermath

Mao became head of state as well as chairman of the Chinese Communist Party. He seemed to become obsessed with making China a major world power and an example of true communism—and suppressed his opposition with brutal punishments. In 1958 Mao deviated from the Soviet economic and political philosophy and declared that in five years China must learn to walk on both legs: the legs of industry and agriculture. This plan, called the "Great Leap Forward," was a devastating disaster for millions of Chinese people. With the promise of a better future, the government encouraged people to work day and night to increase production. In a drive to make steel, people melted all the tools they had, but their primitive methods produced useless steel. To win the favor of high government leaders, local party officials inflated farm output figures. The government took grain from peasants based on these high, false amounts. As a result, the peasants, left with nothing, were forced to eat tree bark, grass roots, and earth. Between 1959 and 1961, thirty million peasants starved to death.

In the early 1960s, Mao stepped down as leader of the government, but still controlled the Chinese Communist Party. The new leaders, more moderate, worked to rebuild the country. They relaxed government controls and China prospered over the next few years. But in 1966 Mao attacked the new leaders, saying they were betraying the radical ideas of the original revolution. He then called on young Chinese to rebel against party officials, starting the Cultural Revolution. Bands of young Chinese, called Red Guards, ransacked museums, libraries, temples, and people's homes. They captured and publicly beat millions of officials, intellectuals, and former landowners. At least 400,000 of these people were beaten to death. The old culture, old customs, old habits, and old ideas of Confucius were eliminated from the Chinese way of life. In his later years, Mao Zedong's judgment was impaired by illness, but he remained the central power in China until his death in 1976.

For More Information

Fitzgerald, C. P. *Mao Tse-tung and China.* New York: Holmes & Meier, 1976.

Heng Liang and Judith Shapiro. *Son of the Revolution.* New York: Vintage Books, 1983.

Mao Tse-tung. *Quotations from Chairman Mao Tse-tung.* Peking: Foreign Languages, 1966.

Marrin, Albert. *Mao Tse-tung and His China.* New York: Viking Penguin, 1989.

Terrill, R. *Mao: A Biography.* New York: Harper, 1980.

Ho Chi Minh

1890-1969

Personal Background

Birth and early life. Ho Chi Minh was a key figure in the history of the southeast Asian nation of Vietnam. His paternal grandmother (his grandmother on his father's side) was the concubine, or mistress, of a man who was already married. Her children from this relationship were of a lower social status than the children the man had fathered with his lawful wife. For this reason, Ho's father, Nguyen Sinh Huy, was a peasant. An extremely intelligent man, Nguyen attended the school in his village when he was a young man. He was so interested in learning that when his teacher moved, Nguyen moved with him. The teacher offered him a job tending buffalo on his farm.

Ho's father eventually married the teacher's eldest daughter (Ho's mother) and together they had three children: a son, Kiem; a daughter, Thanh; and another son, Cung. Cung was the name given to Ho Chi Minh at birth; he changed his name several times during his lifetime. Ho was born in May 1890, in Kim Lien, a village in central Vietnam. While Ho attended school, his father traveled and prepared for examinations to become a mandarin, or public official. When Ho was ten years old, his mother died while giving birth to her fourth child. His father was away at the time, but he returned home to take the children to live with their

▲ **Ho Chi Minh**

Event: Winning independence for North Vietnam.

Role: Ho Chi Minh organized Vietnamese resistance to French rule and then to U.S. support of a divided nation. He became North Vietnam's first president.

mother's parents. They remained with their grandparents through adulthood.

As he matured, Ho became aware of the deep resentment many Vietnamese people held toward the French. France had colonized Vietnam before Ho's birth and exerted great power over the region. (Colonialism is the extension of the power of a nation—in this case France—beyond its own borders.) In the area where Ho grew up, intellectuals began organizing rebellions against the French government and created a center for nationalistic feeling—built upon the struggle for freedom. This environment had a profound effect on Ho, who would one day become Vietnam's first president.

Student and teacher. When he was fifteen years old, Ho went to a Franco-Annamite school. (Franco denotes French influence; Annam is a part of Vietnam.) Like most other schools in Vietnam, it was run by the French and staffed with French and pro-French Vietnamese people. In 1909, having completed his education there, Ho left to take a teaching job at a school in the southern port city of Phan Thiet. This school was owned and operated by a Vietnamese company that manufactured fish sauce and sold groceries. Ho taught French and Vietnamese. He worked there for about eight months, then dropped out of sight.

Saigon. Although historians do not know why Ho left so abruptly, they do know when he left. It was shortly after the Chinese nationalist revolution had succeeded; Ho may have left to pursue the Vietnamese nationalist revolution. The French shut down the school where he taught in Phan Thiet soon after he left—an indication, some say, that the school was already participating in the nationalist movement.

Ho headed for Saigon, where he attended a trade school for commerce and industry for about three months. He then took a job on a cruise ship that sailed between Indochina and Marseilles, France. He worked as the ship's mess boy—under slave-like conditions—from 1911 to 1914.

Experiences in London, Paris, and New York. Before the beginning of World War I in the summer of 1914, Ho moved to

▲ Ho preparing for a mission during the war of resistance against the French colonists. As he matured, Ho became aware of the deep resentment many Vietnamese people held toward the French.

London. His experience as a mess boy helped him win a job assisting Escoffier, a famous pastry chef. But Ho was not concerned with pursuing a career as a renowned chef. His main goal was the achievement of Vietnamese independence. While in London, Ho

53

joined the Overseas Workers Association, an organization of Asian people who protested colonialism. Then, in 1917, he traveled to Paris, where he earned a living retouching photographs. There he changed his name to Nguyen Ai Quoc, meaning "Nguyen the Patriot."

During World War I, Ho moved to the United States and lived in New York City's Harlem. While he was there, he witnessed white on black racism and wrote a pamphlet titled *The Black Race,* noting the similarities between the African American and Vietnamese experiences.

Hope in communism. In 1919, after World War I had ended, Ho returned to France to attend the Versailles Peace Conference, where he intended to present a plan for Vietnam's independence to U.S. president Woodrow Wilson. The Treaty of Versailles focused mainly on the fate of Germany, the aggressor in the war, as determined by the victorious Allied powers, which included Great Britain, France, and the United States. Ho was not even able to get inside the conference auditorium. Feeling shunned by the Allies, he then turned to communism—a political and economic theory advocating the formation of a classless society through the communal ownership of all property—as the best hope for his country.

Ho joined the French Socialist Party in 1920 and later became a founding member of the French Communist Party. He formed the International Colonial Union, which was made up of people from the colonies who were living in Paris. Both the Communist Party and the union opposed colonialism. These organizations provided Ho an opportunity to study models of government that might preserve Vietnam's noncommercial culture. In 1921 he helped to found a new organization, the Intercolonial Union. He also edited the union's weekly newsletter, *The Pariah,* and contributed articles to *The People,* a socialist paper.

Trained in Moscow. The next year Ho traveled to Moscow in the Soviet Union, the center of the communist world. He enrolled in the University of Toilers of the East, where he studied revolutionary techniques and the philosophy of German intellectual Karl Marx. He also joined the Comintern's Southeast Asia Bureau and helped to organize the Peasant International Organi-

▲ Ho was deeply committed to winning independence for Vietnam and ending colonialism in other countries.

zation. In Moscow, Ho became an authority on communist and socialist government and sharpened his leadership skills.

The Soviet Union sent Ho to China in 1925, reportedly to work as a translator in the Soviet consulate. (A consul is a govern-

55

ment official appointed to duties in a foreign country.) His real purpose was to spread information about the communist movement. While in China, Ho organized a group of Vietnamese refugees into the Association of Young Vietnamese Revolutionaries. He also started the League of Oppressed Peoples of Asia. In 1927 Ho returned to Moscow for a short time before moving on to Thailand. He was in constant danger of being imprisoned for his revolutionary activities, so he disguised himself as a Buddhist monk to avoid being captured.

Ho was deeply committed to winning independence for Vietnam and ending colonialism in other countries. To begin reform in southeast Asia, he organized the Indochinese Communist Party in 1930, with its base in Hong Kong. For his communist activities, Ho was arrested, along with a young woman whom he claimed was his niece. She may actually have been his wife or mistress.

Sentenced to death. In 1931 a peasant revolt arose in Vietnam. Even though Ho was living in Hong Kong at the time and therefore was not subject to French rule, the French sentenced him to death. There were false reports that Ho had died sometime between 1931 and 1935. Ho continued his revolutionary activities, living in China until 1932, then moving back to Moscow. He stayed there until 1936, when he returned to China to help **Mao Zedong** (also spelled Mao Tse-tung; see entry) with the communist uprising there. While he was in China, Ho completed his plan for Vietnam's revolution.

Participation:
Winning Independence for North Vietnam

Return to Vietnam. At the age of fifty-one, having been away for thirty years, Ho returned to Vietnam. It was 1941, and in May he founded the Vietminh, a pro-independence, anticolonial organization composed of peasants and scholars. Most of the Vietminh were communists. They were well-organized, had bases in many villages, and were supplied with weapons acquired mostly from China. The Vietminh fought against the Japanese invasion during World War II and against other Vietnamese nationalist groups while continuing a revolution against the French colonial authorities.

In 1942, as the revolutionary movement gained momentum, Ho traveled to China, where he was arrested and jailed. He would spend other periods in prison, but it was during this time that he wrote his famous prison diary, expressing his ideas in poetry. Ho wrote about a hundred poems before his release in 1943.

When he returned to Vietnam, Ho formed a Vietnamese freedom group and entered the government of the Provisional Vietnamese Republic. It was around this time that he adopted the name Ho Chi Minh, which means "he who seeks enlightenment."

The high price of Vietnamese independence. On September 2, 1945, the Vietminh defeated the French at Hanoi. Ho declared Vietnam an independent state and became the new nation's first president. He signed an accord with France in 1946,

which stated that he would be the leader of the Democratic Republic of Vietnam—a free part of the French Union. In the accord, Ho was assigned the task of unifying North and South Vietnam. This was next to impossible, as many Vietnamese people—particularly those living in the South who had converted to Catholicism—resisted communist rule.

Only a few months after the agreement was signed, the French violated its terms. Fighting resumed. Ho went underground for eight years to avoid assassination but still managed to direct the Vietnamese battle against the French in the French Indochina War (1946-54). In 1954, although outnumbered, the Vietminh defeated the French at Dien Bien Phu, a small, seemingly insignificant village in North Vietnam.

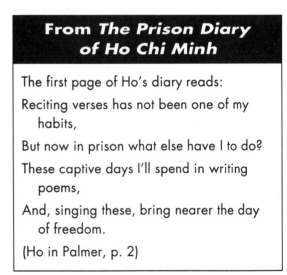

From *The Prison Diary of Ho Chi Minh*

The first page of Ho's diary reads:

Reciting verses has not been one of my habits,

But now in prison what else have I to do?

These captive days I'll spend in writing poems,

And, singing these, bring nearer the day of freedom.

(Ho in Palmer, p. 2)

The Vietminh victory destroyed much of the French resolve to hold on to southeast Asia. At the Geneva Conference of 1954, France had little choice but to realease its already diminished grasp on Southeast Asia. Cambodia and Laos were granted independence, and it was agreed that Vietnam should be divided temporarily. That region was officially split into North and South Vietnam at the seventeenth parallel. Ho signed a cease-fire with the French and in 1954 became president and premier of North Vietnam. About five hundred thousand North Vietnamese fled to South Vietnam. Ho later gave up the premiership to his colleague, Pham Van Dong, but was re-elected president in 1960 by the North Vietnamese National Assembly.

"Uncle Ho"

Ho Chi Minh was known as "Uncle Ho" to those who believed in his vision of an independent Vietnam. He was respected because he was humble and smart. Even those who did not agree with communism agreed that he had done more for the independence of Vietnam than anyone else. Ho was the founder of Vietnamese communism, the leader of Vietnam's movement for independence, and the creator of North Vietnam.

United States versus communism. After the French defeat, the United States tried to contain the spread of communism by supporting the noncommunist government of South Vietnam. Communists in the South were united into the Viet Cong, with village organizations like those Ho Chi Minh had developed successfully in the North. Ho's North Vietnamese government actively supported the Viet Cong, as did the communist government in China. Fighting a guerrilla war, village to village, and bringing fresh supplies and troops through Cambodia along what became known as the Ho Chi Minh Trail, the communists persisted against massive U.S. intervention.

As the struggle dragged on through the mid- to late 1960s, the government of South Vietnam failed and was replaced by a military dictatorship, which seemed to strengthen communist resolve. A surprise attack in central Vietnam in 1968 finally convinced U.S. officials that winning the war would be too costly. Negotiations were begun with Ho Chi Minh to stop the fighting.

Aftermath

On September 3, 1969, after being ill for several weeks, Ho Chi Minh died of a heart attack at the age of seventy-nine. Although Ho did not live to see Vietnam free of all aggressors, he did gain the independence of the Democratic Republic of Vietnam (later known as North Vietnam).

Fenn, Charles. *Ho Chi Minh: A Biographical Introduction.* New York: Charles Scribner's Sons, 1973.

Halberstam, David. *Ho.* New York: Random House, 1971.

Palmer, Aileen. *The Prison Diary of Ho Chi Minh.* New York: Bantam, 1971.

Kwame Nkrumah

1909-1972

Personal Background

Kwame Nkrumah was born September 18, 1909, in the village of Nkroful. A small country settlement populated by the Nzima, a peaceful group of the Akan people, Nkroful sits in the southwestern corner of present-day Ghana, about fifty miles inland on the western coast of Africa.

Early years. The last decades of the nineteenth century saw imperialism, the extension of a nation's power beyond its own borders, rise to new heights. During this time, many European countries acquired territories in Africa and Asia.

At the turn of the twentieth century, Great Britain, which had begun colonization in 1824 and extended its influence to include all of present-day Ghana by 1874, had separated a portion of western coastal Africa and named it the British Gold Coast colony because of its rich supply of gold. Britain soon established a colonial government, set up Christian missions, and began harvesting the gold. By the early twentieth century many tribal African societies were ruled by the laws and beliefs of the British. The land that Nkrumah was born into was in danger of losing its culture along with its independence.

Nkrumah's mother was a trader who sold sugar and rice in the local market. She believed in both the tribal religion based on

▲ **Kwame Nkrumah**

Event: Winning independence for the Gold Coast.

Role: Kwame Nkrumah was the first African-born prime minister in postcolonial Africa. He started the political movement that led to an independent Gold Coast (and eventually to present-day Ghana), establishing policies that promoted the union and strengthening of all African nations.

ancestor worship and the Catholic religion introduced by European missionaries. A soft-spoken, dignified woman, she is said to have punished her son only once—after he spit in a pot of stew she was making for dinner.

Nkrumah's father was a craftsman who traveled from village to village working as a goldsmith. He believed in the traditional religion and customs of his tribe, including a man's right to marry several wives and raise a large family.

Nkrumah spent much of his childhood playing with his half-brothers and half-sisters, helping his mother around the house, and watching the village wildlife. Neither one of his parents could read or write, but they wanted their son to get a good education. When he was nine years old, they sent him to the local Roman Catholic mission school. Nkrumah despised school at first and even ran away in protest, but he came to love learning and later treasured his education. After graduating, he stayed on at the mission school as a pupil-teacher. He was a very dedicated student and teacher and in 1926 earned a scholarship to the government's teacher training college in Accra.

Birth of Nkrumah

Legend has it that when Kwame Nkrumah was born, his mother feared that he was dead. He did not seem to move or breathe for quite some time. Relatives began to pass him around and make loud noises with cymbals to try to wake him up. Finally, one of them stuffed a banana in his mouth. Kwame coughed and took a deep breath, and then they knew that he was indeed alive.

City life. Accra was the capital of the Gold Coast colony. When Nkrumah arrived there to begin school, he was overwhelmed by the mix of people and new ideas in the bustling city. Although the Nkrumah family was well-to-do by the standards of their small village, they were considered simple country folk by the wealthier people of Accra.

Preparing for leadership. In 1928 the Government Training College became part of Achimota College, the Gold Coast's oldest and most prestigious school. Nkrumah fell under the influence of Achimota's vice principal, Kwegyir Aggrey. Wise, charming, and very proud of his African heritage, Aggrey had uncommon courage in expressing his anti-British views. Through his African studies course, Nkrumah was awakened to the politics of

Africa and its European colonizers. He tested his new findings through debate and honed his skills as an orator.

In 1930 Nkrumah left Achimota and took a teaching job at a Roman Catholic junior school in Elmina. For the next few years, he taught at similar schools in various locations. At each school, the young teacher distinguished himself as a leader by organizing teachers' associations and participating in literary societies.

Nkrumah's desire to continue his education led him to study abroad. He was accepted at Lincoln University in Pennsylvania and, after obtaining his travel expenses from a wealthy uncle, set out for America. He began his studies in the fall of 1935 and graduated with a bachelor of arts degree in philosophy four years later. The new graduate then entered Lincoln Theological Seminary. He also enrolled in the University of Pennsylvania graduate school to study philosophy and education. After completing his education, Nkrumah intended to take what he had learned and use it to improve conditions in his homeland.

Nkrumah exposed himself to the finer points of Western economic and political philosophies; his main goal was to work for the independence of the British Gold Coast and the rest of the colonized African nations.

In September 1942 Nkrumah presided over the first meeting of the General Conference of Africans in America. Around the same time, he and another man from the Gold Coast edited a magazine called the *African Interpreter,* which reported the news from colonial Africa. Nkrumah became a popular and effective public speaker about African culture and the destructive nature of colonialism.

During his ten-year stay in the United States, Nkrumah earned degrees in religion and philosophy. He later moved to London to finish work on his doctorate in philosophy and to study law. Nkrumah arrived in London in June 1945—just one month after Germany had surrendered, ending World War II. Europeans everywhere were tired of the war and the years of economic hardship that it brought. The European nations seemed ready to rid themselves of their colonies in Asia and Africa. Nkrumah seized on the opportunity; he abandoned his doctoral studies and instead became involved in radical, freedom-seeking politics.

Political activism. Nkrumah volunteered to help plan and prepare the Fifth Pan-African Congress, a political meeting for African citizens living abroad. The delegates to the congress discussed ways to achieve independence in African nations. Nkrumah and his associates then formed the African National Secretariat. Their purpose was to provide a forum for West Africans to share their concerns and plan for independence. Through study, speechmaking, writing, and organizing, Nkrumah had prepared himself to return home and work for change.

Participation:
Winning Independence for the Gold Coast

Return home. In the fall of 1947 Nkrumah was offered a job with the United Gold Coast Convention (UGCC), a group of conservative West Africans who wanted to control the government and thus improve their business opportunities. Although he disagreed with their philosophy, he accepted the job and returned to the Gold Coast after being away for almost twelve years.

Postwar Africa. Black Africans had fought side by side with European soldiers during World War II. In the postwar years, however, the black majority population in European colonies were subjected to the same kind of racial discrimination they had been forced to endure decades before. In addition, the economies of many West African nations were in a shambles. The people were ready for change.

Nkrumah used his popularity to break away from the UGCC and promote a socialist revolution. He envisioned a new political party for the Gold Coast—the Convention People's Party (CPP)—which he unveiled in June 1949 at a mass meeting in Accra that attracted about sixty thousand people. The party's slogan, "Self-Government Now," became the rallying cry for all segments of Gold Coast society seeking an end to British rule.

General strike. In January 1950 Nkrumah and the CPP organized a workers' strike to protest the political policies of Great Britain. The success of the strike demonstrated the power of the people and gave momentum to the CPP. Eventually members of the party were elected to public office. Little by little, the government came under their control.

At the same time, the British government was working toward leaving the Gold Coast colony. Nkrumah wanted the Gold Coast to be both politically and economically independent, but he knew that this could only happen gradually—and with the cooperation of the British government.

While serving a prison term for his involvement in the strike, Nkrumah was elected to Parliament. After his release in 1951, he was invited to meet with the British governor—the highest official in the Gold Coast colony. The governor was preparing to turn the Gold Coast government over to the West Africans, and he selected Nkrumah as the leader of government business. Nkrumah became prime minister of the Gold Coast colony in 1952, making him the first African-born prime minister on the continent. But Gold Coast independence was not a reality until 1957, when the British government relinquished its control over the colony.

> ## The CPP Plan
>
> Nkrumah was the chairman of the Convention People's Party (CPP), and together with the executive committee he devised a six-point plan:
>
> 1. to fight for full self-government by all constitutional means
> 2. to serve as a political vanguard to stop oppression and establish a democratic government
> 3. to secure and maintain unity between chiefs and people
> 4. to improve conditions for working people in cooperation with trade unions
> 5. to work for the reconstruction of their country to make it a place where a free people would govern themselves
> 6. to assist in the creation of a united and self-governing West Africa. (McKown, p. 57)

Prime Minister. As prime minister of the Gold Coast colony, Nkrumah began to improve transportation, housing, agriculture (specifically the cocoa industry, which became the Gold Coast's biggest export), education, and medical facilities. He imported people from abroad to work in the health care, building, and business fields because the Gold Coast lacked a well-trained workforce. He also sent young Gold Coasters to foreign universities at government expense so that they could return as experts in various areas. Nkrumah consistently focused on independence.

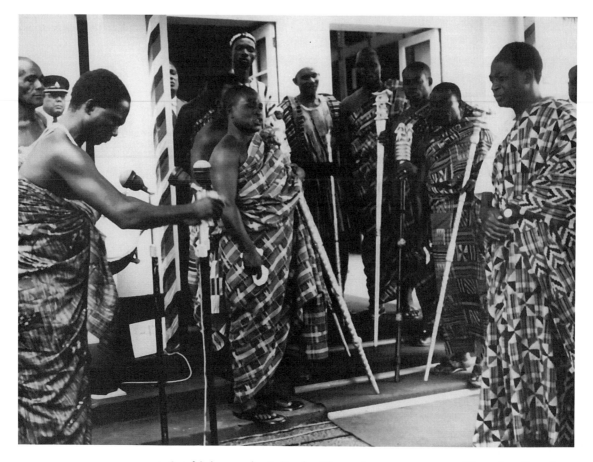

▲ Combining ancient ritual with western ceremony, a Ghanaian linguist pours a libation for Nkrumah (right) and invokes the blessings of the gods upon him and the nation as Nkrumah prepares to enter the Ghana National Assembly in August 1965.

Independence. After independence was granted in March 1957, a portion of neighboring Togoland chose to join the new nation. The Gold Coast colony changed its name to the Republic of Ghana in 1960. Under its new constitution, Nkrumah became Ghana's head of state.

Aftermath

Deposed. From 1960 to 1966 President Nkrumah maintained control of the new republic. The CPP was socialistic and supported the centralization of power and ownership in the government; an opposition party (called the United Party; UP) favored a greater distribution of power and supported capitalist ideals of private ownership and a free competitive market. Nkrumah alienated his Western supporters with many of his actions—such as the nationalization of Ghana's cocoa trade, a move that took control of the trade away from the farmers and placed it in the hands of the state. As he continued to consolidate his own power, his government became more and more dictatorial in nature.

In February 1966, just after Nkrumah had left Ghana for a visit to China and Vietnam, four police officers and four military officials successfully executed a coup (meaning they assumed power). For the next eight years, Nkrumah lived in exile in Guinea, where he was made joint head of state by his friend, Guinean leader Sekou Toure. Nkrumah broadcast messages to Ghana over the "Voice of Revolution" radio network. Even in exile, he remained to his people a symbol of the movement toward African independence.

Death. In 1970 Nkrumah was diagnosed with cancer. By 1972 his condition required expert care. He was being treated at a hospital in Romania when he died that year at the age of sixty-two. Nkrumah was first buried in Guinea, then his body was exhumed months later and buried in his homeland, in the small country village of Nkroful.

For More Information

Jones, Peter. *Kwame Nkrumah and Africa.* London: Hamish Hamilton, 1965.

McKown, Robin. *Nkrumah: A Biography.* New York: Doubleday, 1973.

Nkrumah, Kwame. *Autobiography of Kwame Nkrumah.* Edinburgh: Thomas Nelson and Sons, 1957.

Jawaharlal Nehru

1889-1964

Personal Background

Birth and early life. The Nehru family descended from one of India's highest social classes—the Hindu Kashmiri Brahman. Jawaharlal Nehru's father, Motilal, had inherited his older brother's legal practice and made a good living as an attorney. He was also a member of the Indian National Congress, which had formed in 1885.

Motilal's first wife died shortly after the birth of their only child. The baby died not long after his mother. Later in the 1880s Motilal married his second wife, a fifteen-year-old girl named Swaruprani. Together they lived at the Nehru family estate, Anand Bhavan ("House of Happiness") in Allahabad (meaning "City of God"), a region in north-central India.

In the fall of 1889 Motilal and Swaruprani's first child was born. He was given the name Jawaharlal, which means "precious stone." Jawaharlal was an only child for eleven years; later, Motilal and Swaruprani had two girls, Vijaylakshmi and Krishna.

British India. Great Britain had exerted control over sections of India for nearly three hundred years by the time Nehru was born. During that era, many British citizens immigrated to India. F. T. Brooks, a free-thinking British intellectual and English-language tutor, introduced Nehru to different philosophies and

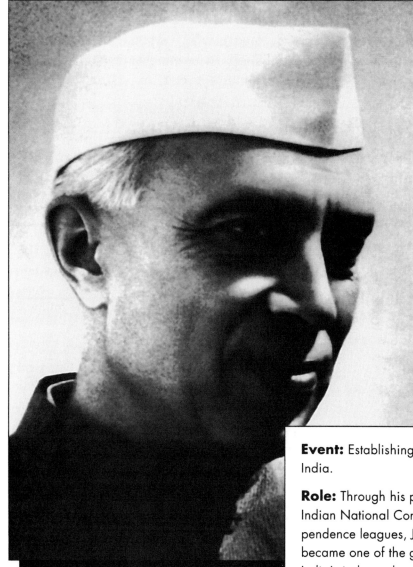

▲ **Jawaharlal Nehru**

Event: Establishing an independent India.

Role: Through his participation in the Indian National Congress and pro-independence leagues, Jawaharlal Nehru became one of the greatest activists for India's independence. He worked with his father and various political figures, including Mohandas Gandhi, to create a strong national movement among India's diverse population. In 1947, when India achieved independence from Great Britain, Nehru became the dominion's first prime minister.

new ways of thinking about life. Nehru's parents objected to these radical ideas because they clashed with basic Hindu beliefs. (Hinduism is an ancient Indian mystical religious tradition that stresses the right way of living.) Even though the Nehrus put an end to the growing relationship between Brooks and their son, young Jawaharlal had already embraced the ideas of his mentor.

At an early age, Nehru became very interested in history and literature. Reading and writing were his two greatest passions. When he was fifteen years old, he moved with his family to England and enrolled in school. For two years he attended Harrow, a British institution with a long, impressive history. Four of Great Britain's prime ministers had been students there. But Nehru never felt that he fit in at Harrow. During his time at the school, he concentrated on history and literature, played quite a bit of chess, and carefully followed current events in India.

Anand Bhavan

The Nehru family home, Anand Bhavan, was a large Victorian-style house. It had lawns for croquet, a rose garden, and a swimming pool, which was very rare in those days. Since his father worked long hours, Jawaharlal spent most of his time with his mother, governesses, servants, and tutors. His mother was an orthodox Hindu, and she raised her son in the practices of the religion.

Nehru's father expected him to become an attorney, although his own ambition was to work in civil service. Reluctantly, he agreed to pursue a career in law—as long as he was allowed to study the subject of his choosing in college. Nehru attended Cambridge University from 1907 to 1910, earning a degree in natural science, with honors. He then studied law at the Inner Temple in London and, after being admitted to the bar in 1912, returned to India to practice law with his father. Nehru was a successful lawyer, but he soon found that he disliked his profession.

Preparation. The Indian National Congress (a political party in India) met in Bankipur in 1912, and Nehru attended the meeting for the first time with his father. At this point in time, the members of the congress did not even consider self-rule as an option for India. This disappointed Nehru. He turned to the anti-war works of British philosopher Bertrand Russell; these ideas deeply influenced Nehru's political position in the years that followed.

Political activism. That same year, Nehru began working to realize his dream of a united, independent India. Though still a full-time attorney, he became active in several pro-independence movements and rallied for an end to British imperialism (the extension of Britain's power beyond its own borders). Nehru's father doubted India's ability to govern itself and therefore opposed his son's support of a national movement for Indian self-rule.

World War I began in the summer of 1914. India supported Great Britain's war efforts by providing supplies and soldiers in exchange for reforms that gave India more control over its own government. But these token reforms left the real power in the hands of Great Britain.

The struggle for independence in India. Great obstacles stood in the way of Indian independence. The nationalist movement (which began in the 1880s and promoted a sense of national strength and consciousness) was weakened by differences in religion, class, and language among the Indian people. The Hindus and the Muslims, members of two distinct religious cultures, strove to maintain their fundamentally different beliefs; a centuries-old strict class system kept property owners and peasants from uniting; and the various peoples of India spoke over two hundred different languages. With so many traditions keeping them divided, it was difficult to imagine the Indian population ever joining together to overcome British rule.

Choosing a Wife

While he was away at school, Nehru's parents began looking for a wife for him. Nehru did not believe in arranged marriages; he wanted to fall in love. Although he tried to discourage his parents, they chose a girl from New Delhi for him. Nehru objected at first, but he later married her.

After friends of the Nehru family were jailed for speaking out against England, Nehru's father came to support the fight for India's independence. In 1919 he financed the publication of the Congress Party newspaper, *The Independent,* and began to work side by side with his son in the nationalist movement.

Indian leader Mohandas Gandhi did much to strengthen the nationalist movement. He became president of the congress in 1920 and founded the Non-Cooperation Movement, which aimed to force Great Britain to give up control of India through nonviolent protests and boycotts of all things British. Nehru became very active in this movement:

I became wholly absorbed and wrapt in the movement, and large numbers of other people did likewise. I gave up all my other associations and contacts, old friends, books, even newspapers, except insofar as they dealt with the work in hand.... In spite of the strength of family bonds, I almost forgot my family, my wife, my daughter. (Nehru in Ali, p. 26)

Participation:
Establishing an Independent India

Civil disobedience. After practicing law for eight years, Nehru pursued political activism full time. He became a vital member of the Congress Party, organizing and leading protests against the British government. He was arrested for the first time in December 1921 for allegedly having illegal contact with a forbidden Afghani group. (Afghanistan is a politically turbulent nation in southern Asia.) He and his father were arrested the next year for their involvement in Gandhi's civil disobedience campaign. (Civil disobedience is a nonviolent method of refusing to obey government policy.) In all, Nehru was jailed nine times and spent a total of thirteen years in prison. Each time he was imprisoned, he read and wrote extensively.

> ### Nehru's Marriage
>
> In 1916, at age twenty-six, Nehru married the sixteen-year-old girl his parents had selected for him four years earlier. Her name was Kamala Kaul. The wedding took place in Delhi and the festivities lasted for nine days. Back home in Allahabad, the celebration continued for almost two more weeks. The Nehrus eventually had a daughter, Indira; in 1966 she became India's first female prime minister.

Nehru's wife, Kamala, contracted tuberculosis in 1925. On the recommendation of doctors, she and their daughter, Indira, moved to Switzerland. Nehru joined them later, then traveled throughout Europe, making contacts with other activists for independence and attending the League of Nations meetings.

General secretary. Nehru was elected general secretary, then president, of the Indian National Congress in 1929. Two years later, he convinced the Congress Working Committee to enact several socialist programs. By 1936 Indian nationalists held the majority of seats in the congress, thanks in large part to the political activities of Nehru.

▲ Nehru with Mohandas Gandhi in July 1946; joined by Gandhi, Nehru succeeded in persuading the British to proceed with plans to make India a separate nation within the British Commonwealth.

World War II began with the German invasion of Czechoslovakia and Poland in 1939. India lent support to the Allied effort (the forces fighting against Germany) by providing supplies and soldiers to Great Britain. But it was not until 1945—after the war had ended, that Great Britain declared its intention to withdraw from India. The following year, Nehru was re-elected president of the Indian National Congress and formed a cabinet to act as India's temporary government. He became India's first prime minister when the nation was granted independence on August 15, 1947. Pakistan was made an independent dominion under the control of the Muslims.

Aftermath

Death of Gandhi. In 1948 Mohandas Gandhi was shot and killed by an assassin who disapproved of Gandhi's tolerance

▲ Nehru addressing the United Nations General Assembly in October 1960; he became India's first prime minister when the nation was granted independence on August 15, 1947.

toward Muslims. His death was just one tragic example of the problems India still had to face following independence. Clashing cultures and boundary disputes rocked the nation. Nehru continued to lead India through policies of neutralism, socialism, and political democracy. He developed programs for economic growth and sought to abolish the strict class system that subdivided India's people. Throughout his life he struggled to shape a unified and prosperous India.

Death of Nehru. In January 1964 Nehru had a stroke. Despite the fact that he was left partially paralyzed, he continued to work for the next five months. On May 27, 1964, at the age of seventy-four, he suffered a heart attack and died eight hours later. In his will, written in 1954, Nehru requested that his body be cremated:

> When I die, I should like my body to be cremated.... A small handful of these ashes should be thrown ... into the Ganga (River) in Allahabad to be carried into the great ocean that washes India's shores. [The rest should be] scattered from the heights over the fields where the peasants of India toil, so that they might mingle with the dust and soil of India and become an indistinguishable part of India. (quoted in Ghose, p. 342)

Nehru's requests reflect his deep love for the country he worked a lifetime to liberate.

For More Information

Ali, Tariq. *An Indian Dynasty: The Story of the Nehru-Gandhi Family.* New York: Putnam, 1985.

Ghose, Sankar. *Jawaharlal Nehru: A Biography.* New Delhi: Allied, 1993.

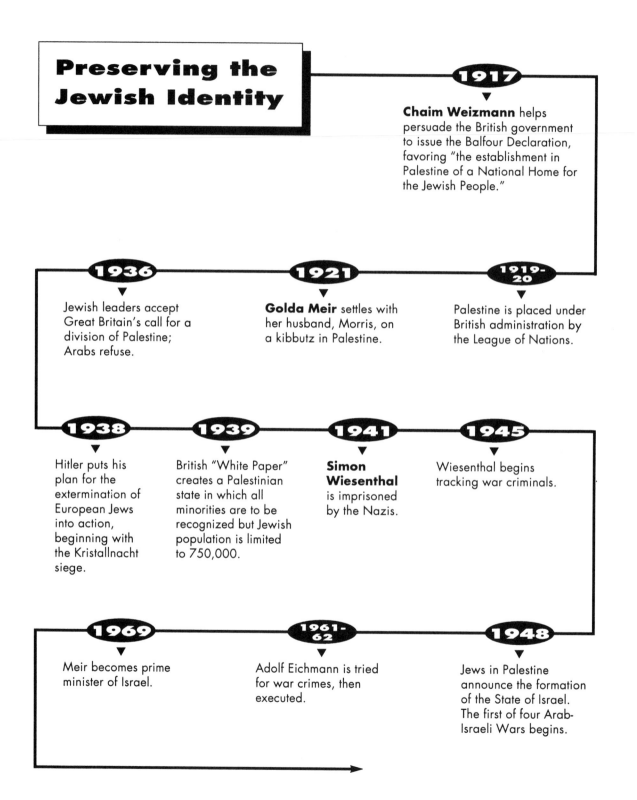

Preserving the Jewish Identity

1917
Chaim Weizmann helps persuade the British government to issue the Balfour Declaration, favoring "the establishment in Palestine of a National Home for the Jewish People."

1936
Jewish leaders accept Great Britain's call for a division of Palestine; Arabs refuse.

1921
Golda Meir settles with her husband, Morris, on a kibbutz in Palestine.

1919-20
Palestine is placed under British administration by the League of Nations.

1938
Hitler puts his plan for the extermination of European Jews into action, beginning with the Kristallnacht siege.

1939
British "White Paper" creates a Palestinian state in which all minorities are to be recognized but Jewish population is limited to 750,000.

1941
Simon Wiesenthal is imprisoned by the Nazis.

1945
Wiesenthal begins tracking war criminals.

1969
Meir becomes prime minister of Israel.

1961-62
Adolf Eichmann is tried for war crimes, then executed.

1948
Jews in Palestine announce the formation of the State of Israel. The first of four Arab-Israeli Wars begins.

PRESERVING THE JEWISH IDENTITY

Scathing excerpts from *Mein Kampf,* Adolf Hitler's autobiography, reflect the growing anti-Jewish sentiment that came to dominate the thoughts and actions of Nazi Germany's rulers from the 1930s:

As always [when wondering about the ethnicity of a stranger], I began to try to relieve my doubts by books. For a few pennies I bought the first anti-Semitic pamphlet of my life....

In a short time I was made more thoughtful than ever by my slowly rising insight into the type of activity carried on by the Jews in certain fields.

Was there any form of filth or profligacy [self-indulgence], particularly in cultural life, without at least one Jew involved in it?

If you cut even cautiously into such an abscess, you found, like a maggot in a rotting body, often dazzled by the sudden light—a kike!

What had to be reckoned heavily against the Jews in my eyes was when I became acquainted with their activities in the press, art, literature, and the theater.

The fact that nine-tenths of all literary filth, artistic trash, and theatrical idiocy can be set to the account of a people constituting hardly one hundredth of all the country's inhabitants could simply not be talked away; it was the plain truth.

Unfortunately, anti-Semitism did not originate with Hitler, nor did he stand alone. Anti-Jewish sentiment had been rampant in Europe for hundreds of years and seemed to increase in its intensity toward the close of the nineteenth century, particularly in Eastern Europe. With the approval or direction of the czars (Russia's absolute rulers), Russian soldiers carried out pogroms, or massacres, in which Jewish settlements were raided and Jewish people were killed. Jews faced inequities in housing and employment, and laws regulating anti-Semitic views did little to relieve their plight. Throughout Europe, there seemed to be nowhere that a Jewish person could claim equal citizenship with non-Jews, not even in those towns designated for Jewish residence.

Zionism. At the end of the nineteenth century, after at least four hundred years of persecution, European Jews began to think and talk about establishing a separate homeland where they could live in peace. Some non-Jewish politicians offered them nearly uninhabitable lands in countries that were sparsely populated. But the Jews were committed to claiming the Middle Eastern region of Palestine. Thousands of years earlier, the Jews had moved along the Mediterranean coast to capture and settle this land.

After Theodor Herzl wrote about a homeland for the Jews in 1896, support for the effort grew. Herzl organized a Zionist movement, so named because a mountain near old Jerusalem (which is now the capital of Israel) bore the name Zion. First Herzl and then **Chaim Weizmann** and others nurtured the idea of a Jewish state in Palestine. As many as three thousand Jews moved into their ancient land each year throughout the early twentieth century.

Weizmann's work as a chemist brought him in contact with many British leaders. In 1917 he saw the opportunity to secure British blessings for the formation of a Jewish state. British authorities went on record as favoring the idea, and Britain was given a United Nations mandate to manage Palestine. Still, Weizmann and several other strong and dedicated Jewish leaders had to wait for the end of another world war before establishing their own independent nation—Israel—with Weizmann as its first president.

European anti-Semitism. Adolf Hitler had taken command of much of Europe before and during World War II. Besides his own hatred of the Jews, the smoldering anti-Jewish sentiment that pervaded Europe added to his power. The hatred festered and resulted in a plan to eliminate all Jewish people in Europe and throughout the world. Hitler and his unscrupulous henchmen almost succeeded. Six million—nearly half of the European Jews—were destroyed before Allied forces (including those of Great Britain, France, the United States, and the Soviet Union) could stop the madness.

One of those Jews who survived the German prisons (mostly, say historians, because he was too weak to work but too stubborn to die) was **Simon Wiesenthal.** After the war, Wiesenthal worked to perpetuate the memory of the Holocaust victims and bring their persecutors to justice. He remains a constant reminder that such inhumanities cannot and will not ever be tolerated again.

The end of the war and the founding of a Jewish homeland did not bring peace for the Jews. Israel has long been at odds—if not at war—with its Arab neighbors. One of the early settlers, and perhaps Israel's most powerful woman pioneer, was **Golda Meir.** Born in Russia and raised in the United States, Meir moved to Palestine as a young woman to live the pioneer life of a kibbutz worker. From this beginning she rose to power in the Israeli government and served as the nation's prime minister during some of its darkest hours of conflict with its Arab neighbors. Meir came to represent the determination and strength that held Israel together and helped to develop it into a thriving homeland for the Jewish people.

Chaim Weizmann

1874-1952

Personal Background

Chaim Azriel Weizmann was born on November 7, 1874, in Motol, a small town in present-day Belarus in western Russia. His father, a timber merchant, was an orthodox Jew and a Malkal, or modernizer, who belonged to a movement that worked toward a Jewish cultural renaissance.

After receiving his primary education in Motol, Chaim was sent to Pinsk, a city about twenty-five miles away, where he attended a *realschule,* or high school. Although most Jews in the region spoke only Yiddish—a language based on tenth-century German with Hebrew and Slavic influences—Chaim's father insisted that he learn Russian in order to broaden his educational and career opportunities. By the time he reached his teens, Weizmann had mastered the Russian language and was reading the works of nineteenth-century Russian novelists Nikolai Gogol, Feodor Dostoyevsky, and Ivan Turgenev. At the same time, he became an expert in the study of chemistry. Soon he was giving private lessons to wealthier Jews and adding to his family's modest income.

Berlin and science. Weizmann left Russia's oppressive atmosphere and headed for Germany to pursue his higher education. To support himself, he taught Russian and Hebrew at a Jewish school in Pfungstadt while living in the nearby southwest German town of Darmstadt. About a year later, Weizmann was accepted at

▲ **Chaim Weizmann**

Event: Securing approval for an independent Palestine.

Role: Chaim Weizmann was a prominent leader in the Zionist movement, which sought to recover a homeland in Palestine for the Jewish people. He played a key role in the passage of the Balfour Declaration and the establishment of the state of Israel.

the prestigious Technical College—one of the best science schools in Europe—located in Charlottenburg, a suburb of Berlin.

In Berlin, Weizmann associated with a group of Jewish intellectuals who were calling for a reestablishment of the ancient Jewish nation. The Jewish people had been slaves in Egypt before being led out of bondage by Moses more than a thousand years before the birth of Christ. Since then, Jews have waged on ongoing battle for peace in the land along the River Jordan, which they call home.

Persecution of the Jews

Weizmann grew up in an atmosphere in which Jews were persecuted. Czarist authorities (representatives of the czar, or absolute ruler, of Russia) placed numerous restrictions on the Jewish people. For example, they were only allowed to attend secondary schools and universities under a quota system; they were subjected to segregated housing rules (forced to live only in certain communities such as Pinsk, located near vast Ukrainian swamps); and they faced ongoing harassment and abuse. Pogroms—organized and officially approved raids during which Jews were beaten, robbed, or killed—were frequent occurrences.

The Jewish claim to Palestine. Weizmann had shown an interest in Jewish nationalism (a sense of national consciousness and loyalty) from an early age. When he was only eleven years old, he wrote a letter expressing his belief that the kings of the world were bent on destroying the Jews and that only England could help the Jews return to Palestine, their historic homeland, where they would rise again. (Palestine is a region in the Middle East bordered on the west by the Mediterranean Sea and to the east by the Dead Sea. It has long been the scene of fighting between the Arab and Israeli peoples—especially along the West Bank area near the River Jordan.) Around 1890 Weizmann joined an organization called the "Lovers of Zion"—Mount Zion is the site of Jerusalem, the capital of Israel—which advocated a Jewish homeland in Palestine.

Theodor Herzl and Zionism. In 1895 Theodor Herzl, a Hungarian Jewish journalist living in Paris, wrote a pamphlet calling for the creation of a Jewish state. To Weizmann, who was studying in Charlottenburg at the time, Herzl's proposal came "like a bolt from the blue" (Johnson, p. 399). Weizmann soon became active in the movement and attended the second Zionist Congress in 1898.

Meanwhile, Weizmann continued his education. In 1897 he entered the University of Freiburg (or Fribourg) in Switzerland, earning his doctorate within two years. From this point on, he would divide his time between scientific research and Zionist politics.

Various Zionist leaders disagreed over where and how a Jewish nation should be established. Weizmann supported the creation of Jewish cultural and educational institutions in Palestine, where small Jewish communities had existed for centuries. Weizmann believed that by organizing and financing Jewish immigration to Palestine and setting up Jewish institutions there, these small communities might increase their strength, grow, and flourish.

A Ugandan homeland. Herzl's lobbying activities paid off when the British offered the Zionists territory in Uganda (a country in East Africa) to set up a Jewish state. At the 1903 Zionist Congress, Herzl pushed for acceptance of the Ugandan proposal. But because the Jews had no religious or historical connection with Uganda, Weizmann and many other delegates—most of them from Eastern Europe—strongly opposed the idea. Due to widespread opposition among Zionists and others who understood the project to be impractical, a Ugandan homeland for the Jews never materialized.

Zionism and Palestine

The first Zionist Congress met in 1897 in Switzerland. It called for creating a home in Palestine—secured by public law—for the Jewish people. Taking action on this idea, about one thousand Jews migrated to Palestine in 1900 and formed small communities there. This trend grew as Weizmann began taking over leadership of the Zionist movement after Herzl's death. About three thousand Jews moved to Palestine every year from 1904 to the beginning of World War I.

In 1904 Weizmann accepted a faculty position at the University of Manchester in England. Even as a junior member of the faculty with a limited knowledge of English, he was readily accepted by the students and staff. He found financial backing for his scientific work and earned another advanced degree in science in 1910. That same year, Weizmann became a citizen of England.

Meeting Lord Balfour. Weizmann assumed control of the Zionist movement after Theodor Herzl's death in 1904. He continued his Zionist activities and began making contacts among England's political elite. In late 1905 Weizmann met with British statesman Lord Arthur Balfour to explain the Jewish people's

▲ Weizmann and fellow Zionist and scientist Albert Einstein; from 1899 on, Weizmann would divide his time between scientific research and Zionist politics.

plight and the resulting Zionist movement. Balfour was convinced that the Jews were an exploited and misunderstood people who needed a homeland.

Participation: Securing Approval for an Independent Palestine

Arguments for a Jewish nation. In 1914 the Ottoman (or

Turkish) Empire, which controlled Palestine, entered World War I on the side of the Central Powers led by Germany. Weizmann, who believed England and the rest of the Allied Powers would eventually win the war, began lobbying British officials to make the creation of a Jewish state in Palestine one of England's war aims. He argued that a friendly Jewish state under British protection would serve as an asset to the British empire by guarding the Suez Canal and the route to India. At the same time, Herbert Samuel, a Zionist and a government minister, campaigned for a Jewish state under British government. But the British Foreign Office sought to gain favor with the Arabs, and War Minister Horatio H. Kitchener believed that "Palestine would be of no value to us [the British] whatsoever" (Johnson, p. 427). Still, as World War I progressed, Samuel and Weizmann continued to press for British recognition of Zionism.

World War I. After 1915 events began to turn in the Zionists' favor. David Lloyd George became war minister. Balfour, whom Weizmann had won over, became foreign secretary. Meanwhile, British forces in the eastern Mediterranean, in the vicinity of Palestine, were being strengthened. It appeared that the time was ripe for the government to declare its support for a Jewish state in Palestine.

> ## Weizmann in England
>
> Weizmann began teaching chemistry at England's University of Manchester in 1904. The pay was modest—three pounds a week—and he found himself working in a small basement laboratory. In addition, he felt lonesome, living in a strange country and cut off from his friends. But Weizmann's fiancée, Vera Chatzmann, a Russian Jew whom he had met in Switzerland, soon joined him. A qualified medical doctor in continental Europe, Chatzmann began studying for a degree that would allow her to practice medicine in England. They were married in 1906.

Despite powerful friends in the government, Weizmann and his fellow Zionists still faced several formidable obstacles. Many if not most Jews in Western Europe were satisfied with their status as citizens of their respective countries. One of Lloyd George's cabinet members, Edwin Montagu, who served as secretary of state for India, was a leading anti-Zionist Jew.

During World War I, the British had what seemed to be more pressing objectives. They felt a need to support Palestine's Arab majority, whom they were trying to incite against the Turks; they had also promised part of Palestine to the French in a secret

▲ Weizmann talks with female Israeli soldiers in 1948; he had said that the Zionists hoped to "build up gradually a nationality which would be as Jewish as the French nation was French and the British nation was British"

treaty. Under the cloud of these concerns, a political committee set up by the Zionists submitted a draft proposal to the British government in July 1917. According to the terms of the declaration, the government would agree to "accept the principle of recognizing Palestine as the National Home of the Jewish People" (Fyvel, p. 158). This document called for Jewish self-rule and unrestricted immigration. The initial draft of the declaration was not approved by the British cabinet.

After considerable political maneuvering on Weizmann's part, the proposal was reconsidered in October 1917. The cabinet heatedly debated the possible consequences of the declaration, then voted that a new draft be submitted and reviewed by Zionist and anti-Zionist Jewish groups as well as by U.S. president Woodrow Wilson. Later, in a letter to Lloyd George, Weizmann angrily denounced the anti-Zionist Jews, whom he blamed for blocking the declaration. Zionists and other Jewish groups continued to rally in favor of Palestine as a national home for the Jews.

British commitment. Government officials submitted a new draft designed to meet non-Zionist Jewish and potential Arab objections. The revised document called for:

1) establishing a "national home for the Jewish race" in Palestine

2) protecting the civil rights of the "existing non-Jewish" (mainly Arab) communities in Palestine

3) protecting the rights and political status of Jews in any other country "who are fully contented with their existing nationality" (thereby defusing the divided loyalty issue). (Fyvel, p. 163)

Finalizing the Balfour Declaration. Under the revised proposal, Palestine itself was no longer described as the national home for the Jews. Instead, the declaration called for the national home to be located within the borders of Palestine, implying that the Jews would have to share control over Palestine with the Arabs. There was also no mention of unrestricted Jewish immigration. On October 31, the cabinet approved the declaration, although some members maintained that Palestine—an impoverished region with an overwhelming Arab majority—offered little prospect for successful Jewish colonization.

After the declaration was approved, Sir Mark Sykes, likening it to a newborn baby, told Weizmann, who was waiting outside, "Dr. Weizmann, it's a boy" (Fyvel, p. 165). The declaration was then made public in the form of a letter from Balfour to Lord Walter Rothchild, a noted biologist who was considered the head of the

> ## Weizmann and British Politicians
>
> Through Henry Sacher, a Zionist who was a London journalist, Weizmann came to know C. P. Scott, the influential editor of the *Manchester Guardian*. By 1913 the persuasive Weizmann had converted Scott to the Zionist cause. Through Scott, Weizmann met important British politicians, including Winston Churchill and David Lloyd George, both of whom later served as British prime minister and became influential supporters of Zionism.

Jewish community in England. Thus it became known as the Balfour Declaration.

Weizmann was disappointed that the final declaration was less forceful than the original draft. Even so, as one writer noted, "the Balfour Declaration gave to the prayerful multitudes their signal to return to the homeland" (Litvinoff, p. 154). Weizmann shared the credit for bringing about the Balfour Declaration with Herbert Samuel, who lobbied for it behind the scenes within the government. Nevertheless, General Jan C. Smuts, a prominent figure within the British government, said later, "It was Dr. Weizmann who persuaded us" to support a Jewish homeland (Fyvel, p. 143).

Aftermath

Zionism. Weizmann headed the Zionist Organization, the main Zionist group, on and off until 1946. In 1919, after the close of World War I, he was invited to the Versailles Peace Conference to present his views on the terms of the war treaty. At the conference, he is said to have told the American secretary of state, Robert Lansing, that the Zionists hoped to "build up gradually a nationality which would be as Jewish as the French nation was French and the British nation was British" (Berlin, p. 39).

British resolve. After World War I, the League of Nations gave England the responsibility to oversee the establishment of a government in Palestine, but its commitment to a Jewish homeland waned after Lord George Nathaniel Curzon became foreign secretary later in 1919. Weizmann continued to push the British government to allow increased Jewish immigration, mostly to no avail. During the 1930s he raised funds for the Zionist cause and organized aid for refugees from Germany. Internal struggles among members of the Zionist community were compounded by tensions between Arabs and Jews. Still, in 1921 Weizmann laid the cornerstone for Hebrew University in Jerusalem. The university opened in 1925, fulfilling one of his greatest aspirations.

Scientific research

Besides his Zionist activities, Weizmann continued to build his reputation as a researcher in bacteriology and biochemistry. He was a frequent visitor to the Pasteur Institute in Paris. He also became a respected lecturer.

During World War II, England continued to pursue a pro-Arab policy despite the leadership of Winston Churchill, a Zionist sympathizer. The British position brought Weizmann much frustration, and he turned to the United States for help, making numerous trips there during the war to push the Zionist cause. While in the United States, he continued his scientific activities and patented a method of producing synthetic rubber.

Palestine after World War II. After the war, Weizmann called on the Allies to allow tens of thousands of European Jewish refugees to immigrate to Palestine. Around this time, intense fighting broke out between Jewish rebels and the British. In 1947 Britain relinquished its ties to Palestine. Palestine would then be divided between the Arabs and the Jews.

The United States was ready to award the southern Negev Desert to the Arabs. Weizmann, who was by this time sick and losing his eyesight, flew to Washington to persuade American officials against giving the territory to the Arabs. To do so would have cut the Jewish state off from the Red Sea, thereby limiting access to the Indian Ocean and the Far East. Once again, Weizmann's persuasiveness prevailed, and the southern Negev was awarded to the Jews.

> ## Help from the Military
>
> In 1916 Winston Churchill, the First Lord of the Admiralty, asked Weizmann if he could produce thirty thousand tons of acetone, which was needed for naval guns, by using a fermentation process that he had developed. Weizmann moved from Manchester to London and began work on the project. The eventual success of the acetone project enhanced Weizmann's prestige.

Israel at last declared its independence in 1948, and Weizmann became the country's first president. He died there in 1952.

For More Information

Berlin, Isaiah. "The Biographical Facts." In *Chaim Weizmann,* edited by Meyer W. Weisgal and Joel Carmichael. New York: Atheneum, 1963.

Fyvel, T. R. "Weizmann and the Balfour Declaration." In *Chaim Weizmann,* edited by Meyer W. Weisgal and Joel Carmichael. New York: Atheneum, 1963.

Johnson, Paul. *A History of the Jews.* New York: Harper, 1987.

Litvinoff, Barnet. *To the House of Their Fathers: A History of Zionism.* New York: Frederick A. Praeger, 1965.

Golda Meir

1898-1978

Personal Background

A bleak childhood. In her autobiography, *My Life,* Golda Meir sums up her dismal early childhood:

> It is sad that I have very few happy or even pleasant memories of this time [her first eight years]. The isolated episodes that have stayed with me throughout the past seventy years have to do mostly with the terrible hardships my family suffered, with poverty, cold, hunger, and fear, and I suppose my recollection of being frightened is the clearest of all my memories. (Meir 1975, p. 13)

Meir was born Goldie Mabovitch in 1898 in Ukraine. (Ukraine is a southeast European republic. It was a part of Russia for centuries, then became part of the Union of Soviet Socialist Republics [U.S.S.R. or Soviet Union] in 1922. Following the breakup of the Soviet Union in 1991, Ukraine declared its independence.) Jews in Russia led extremely difficult lives in the 1890s. Meir's parents—Moshe Yitzhak Mabovitch, a carpenter, and his wife, Blume Neidotz—had met in Pinsk, a city near the great swamps of Ukraine. The first Mabovitch daughter, Sheyna, was born at Pinsk, but the town was small and poor—almost too poor to support a skilled carpenter. When Sheyna was still quite young, the family moved to Kiev, the Ukrainian capital.

▲ Golda Meir

Event: Forming the independent state of Israel.

Role: Golda Meir was a powerful figure in the Zionist cause, which sought to establish a Jewish homeland in Palestine. Her hard work and dedication resulted in significant advances in Jewish leadership under the British. One of the original twenty-five Jewish leaders to sign Israel's proclamation of independence on May 14, 1948, Meir later served as her nation's prime minister.

Kiev was a large town with more opportunities for work, but it was not a region of Russia in which Jews were supposed to live. Nevertheless, Moshe found occasional work there, and Blume gave birth to their second daughter, Goldie, on May 2, 1898.

Pinsk. The Mabovitch family faced serious economic problems until a wealthy Kiev family hired Blume to nurse their child. In 1903 Moshe decided to go to America to seek his fortune. The rest of the family—including Blume, Sheyna, Goldie, and baby Zipke—moved back to Pinsk, where Goldie's grandparents lived. For three years, the young children were surrounded by the love of their mother and grandparents. But they lived in constant fear of the great swamps that bordered the town and the fierce Cossacks (members of military organizations active in southern Russia and Ukraine) who frequently thundered through Pinsk as the enforcers of the Russian czar (or ruler). Around this time, with the help of her elder sister, Sheyna, Goldie learned to read and write. Meanwhile, Moshe Mabovitch secured a job in the United States, saved some money, and sent for his family to join him in Milwaukee.

Sheyna. Sheyna Mabovitch was a well-educated seventeen year old when the family sailed for America. She had already begun to speak for Zionism (the idea of founding a separate Jewish state) and for socialism, even though the Cossacks always threatened anyone who was thought to favor ideas not approved by the czar.

The Mabovitch family had not been in Milwaukee long before Sheyna was active in the Socialist Labor Party. (Socialists advocate the creation of a more equal society, usually through removal of the right to private ownership of property.) Having decided to become a teacher during high school, Goldie turned to her older sister for help. Goldie's father was opposed to her choice of a career in education. She rebelled by running away from home. By then, Sheyna was married and living in Denver, Colorado. Goldie went there only to find that her sister and brother-in-law were stricter and more demanding than her parents.

Goldie returned to Milwaukee after a year. While she was away, Moshe had softened his attitude about her plans to become a teacher. Goldie graduated from high school, attended a teachers' seminary, and then began work as a teacher and assistant librarian. This work took her from Milwaukee to Chicago and New York during World War I. Earlier, while staying with Sheyna in Denver, Goldie had met and fallen in love with Morris Myerson, a young activist. Myerson proposed to her, but they weren't married until 1917.

Palestine and Ben-Gurion. Goldie Myerson had a keen interest in the continuing struggle for a Jewish homeland. She was aware that a movement to establish a Jewish presence in Palestine had begun even before her own birth. It had been a major subject among European Jews since the 1880s, when many Jews were forced to flee Russia. About twenty-five thousand of them had migrated to Palestine. In 1905 Aaron David Gordon settled at the deserted tip of the Sea of Galilee and started Deganya, the first communal farm (or kibbutz). Gradually the Jews established small holds in Palestine. Then, in 1916, the sultan of the Ottoman (Turkish) empire announced the eviction of all Jews from Palestine.

That same year, David Ben-Gurion, a Polish-born statesman and labor leader who had immigrated to Palestine, went to Milwaukee during a visit to the United States to recruit candidates for a Jewish legion. Myerson listened to him speak and began to think about independence for Jews in their old homeland.

Family Strain

Morris and Goldie loved each other deeply—so deeply that when her commitment to Zionism resulted in a desire to move to Palestine, he agreed, and when Morris demanded that they part with the kibbutz she loved, she agreed. The couple raised two children, Menachem and Sarah. But Goldie's activities on the part of a Jewish Palestine eventually put a strain on their relationship. Morris and Goldie later decided to live separately. Even so, they loved and respected each other and remained legally married until Morris's death in 1951.

Pioneering activist. Myerson soon determined that the only place for her to work meaningfully for the Jewish people was in Palestine. In 1921 she and her husband moved there and were soon accepted into Merhavia, a beginning kibbutz about ten miles from Nazareth. Goldie felt at home in her new surroundings almost immediately, but Morris had a much more difficult time adjusting to communal life. Within three years he was demanding that the family move to a city.

The Myerson family moved to Tel Aviv (the capital of Israel until 1950), where Goldie took in laundry and Morris worked as a bookkeeper. Goldie Myerson soon became involved with Mapai, the Jewish Labor Party, and with Histadrut, an organization that oversaw all labor unions in Palestine. Soon after her initial involvement, she began to rise to positions of importance in the Jewish Agency (the Jewish advisory board under British rule in Palestine) and the World Zionist Organization.

In 1924 Myerson was named treasurer of Solel Boneh, the Histadrut's ministry of public works. It was a powerful position: Solel Boneh handled all the contracting for public works (construction of roads, schools, and the like for public use) in Palestine. Soon she was traveling back and forth between Tel Aviv and Jerusalem, making speeches for Histadrut, and raising money for the union. In 1934 she was asked to join the Va'ad Hapoel, the executive committee of Histadrut, and became chairperson of the union's sick fund.

Myerson was a gifted speaker: always clear, to the point, and well prepared. Her extraordinary communication skills made her an excellent fund-raiser. In 1937 Histadrut sent her to the United States to raise money for the improvement of the Jewish port at Tel Aviv.

Participation:
Forming the Independent State of Israel

Preparing for independence. Jewish leaders headed by **Chaim Weizmann** (see entry) and David Ben-Gurion did not waver in their determination to form a homeland for Jews, and progress continued. Back in 1909 the city of Tel Aviv had been established as a Jewish seaport next to the ancient port of Jaffa. The Jewish Agency had been founded under the British protectorate to champion Jewish causes in Palestine and advise the British governors. Histadrut had become a leader in planning for Jewish communities and in raising money needed for construction and protection against the raiding Arabs.

As the United Nations and Great Britain prepared to resolve the Jewish-Arab conflict after World War II, pressure increased to raise funds for a Jewish militia and for much-needed public works projects. In 1948 Myerson made another trip to the United States, this time with two goals: to ask the U.S. government to relieve an embargo (or restriction on commerce) that was preventing Jews in Palestine from preparing their defense; and to raise $50 million for Histadrut's building programs. Her moving speeches and straightforward description of the tense situation in Palestine won the hearts of America's Jewish population. Myerson returned home with pledges for more than $100 million. This money would help greatly when Arabs violently protested the next courageous move toward the formation of a Jewish state.

Proclamation of independence. By 1948 Britain had announced that it was withdrawing from Palestine and requested that the United Nations take over the protectorate. Jewish leaders, who saw this as both an opportunity and a threat, moved to fulfill their longtime goal of forming a Jewish homeland. As a member of the Jewish Agency, Myerson helped write a statement proclaiming the formation of a Jewish state. She was then selected to make a secret visit to King Abdullah of Transjordania (a section of land east of the River Jordan) in hopes that he would calm the Arab League's resistance against the Jews.

When that mission failed, Myerson returned to Tel Aviv, and the Jewish leaders decided to go ahead with plans for the establishment and defense of a Jewish

Great Britain and the Jews of Palestine

After Great Britain took Palestine from the Ottoman Empire in 1917, Lord Balfour, the seventy-year-old British foreign minister, issued a statement approving a Jewish state in Palestine. The Jews rejoiced in this Balfour Declaration, especially when, after the war, the League of Nations approved of the idea and Great Britain was named overseer of Palestine. Britain and the League of Nations proposed that Palestine be split into two states: one Jewish and one Arab. But the Arab world was very much opposed to the creation of a Jewish state. By 1936 Arabs and Jews were engaged in a heated battle as Arabs sought to oust Jews from their Palestinian settlements.

Arab raids and Jewish resistance increased until Britain bowed to Arab pressure in 1939 and issued a "White Paper," which advocated severe restrictions on Jewish migration to Palestine—thereby reversing the position of the Balfour Declaration. Jews objected to the new restraints, and in 1947 the United Nations resurrected the proposal that Palestine be divided between Jews and Arabs. Again, the Arabs refused, but by this time Britain had grown weary of its responsibilities in Palestine. The next year Great Britain withdrew from the area, leaving the Arabs, the Jews, and the United Nations to iron out the confusion.

homeland. The heads of Haganah, the Jewish militia, were consulted, and they optimistically estimated that chances for success in battle with the Arabs were about even. (There were 650,000 Jews in Palestine and a million Arabs. Along the proposed borders of the new Jewish state, armies of five Arab nations were mounting an attack.)

On May 14, 1948, Myerson and the other members of a People's Council met to decide on a name for the new state and to prepare a declaration of independence. That afternoon, the mass of people who had gathered for the event sang the new Jewish national anthem, *Hatikvah*. Then Ben-Gurion, a key figure in the Zionist movement, rose to announce the creation of a new nation.

We the members of the National Council ... by virtue of our natural and historic right and of the resolution of the General Assembly of the United Nations, do hereby proclaim the establishment of a Jewish state in the Land of Israel—the State of Israel. (Ben-Gurion in Meir 1975, p. 226)

Goldie Myerson described her own feelings about the event:

The State of Israel! My eyes filled with tears, and my hands shook. We had done it. We had brought the Jewish state into existence—and I, Goldie Mabovitch Myerson, had lived to see the day. Whatever happened now, whatever price any of us would have to pay for it, we had re-created the Jewish national home. (Meir 1975, p. 226)

Goldie Mabovitch Myerson was one of the twenty-five Jewish leaders to sign the new proclamation that day.

Aftermath

War. Almost immediately, Arab armies invaded the new state; the Israelis resisted. The first of what came to be known as the Arab-Israeli Wars dragged on as many of the world's nations recognized the new state. Finally, the United Nations interceded and forced a cease-fire between the Jews and the Arabs. Never-

▲ Golda Meir at a press conference in New York City, September 17, 1970. Meir led Israel through a strong building program and was a powerful leader, but her rule was marred by an incident for which she took total responsibility.

theless, Arab resistance to Israel persisted throughout most of the twentieth century.

Myerson to Meir. Myerson was appointed to several important Israeli political positions. She became the new nation's first ambassador to the Soviet Union in 1948. From 1949 (when she was elected to the Knesset, the Parliament of Israel) to 1956 she served as minister of labor and social security in the Israeli cabinet.

Then, in 1956, Israeli prime minister David Ben-Gurion demanded that Goldie change her surname to a more Hebrew form. Known from then on as Golda Meir, she filled the important post of minister of foreign affairs, a sort of secretary of state, from 1956 to 1966. At age sixty-eight, she announced her retirement from government but remained active when the Arab nations again massed their armies to attack.

This time Egypt and Syria led the charge. In June 1967, however, a well-prepared Israeli army attacked instead. In the famous Six Day War, the Arabs were thoroughly defeated and lost key military lands—including the West Bank of the River Jordan—to Israel.

Prime minister. Levi Eshkol became Israel's prime minister after Ben-Gurion's retirement in 1963. Eshkol died of a heart attack in 1969. The choice of a replacement fell between Minister of Defense Moshe Dayan and Deputy Prime Minister Yigal Allon. Choosing either of the two threatened to divide the country's leadership. Instead, influential government officials, including Allon, pressed for Golda Meir to come out of retirement and head the government. In 1969 she became prime minister and served in that capacity for five years. Meir led Israel through a strong building program to accommodate the free admission of any Jews who wished to migrate there. She was a powerful leader in economics and in resistance to the Arabs, but her rule was marred by an Arab incident for which she took total responsibility.

The Yom Kippur War. In 1973 Egypt, Syria, and other Arab nations again massed their armies to attack Israel. Meir and her cabinet watched the buildup, and her military consultants, including Moshe Dayan, advised that the Israeli army was well prepared to resist invasion. The Arab leaders waited until the Jewish people's most holy day, Yom Kippur, to launch an attack. Arab soldiers were heavily armed with Soviet weapons. Many Israeli soldiers were at home observing the holy day. The invasion—referred to as the Yom Kippur War or the Fourth Arab-Israeli War—drove the Israeli Army deep into its own land before massive armaments arrived from the United States and a counter-battle began. Again foreign nations had to intercede to put a stop to the fighting. Although Meir acted on the advice of her military leaders, she was blamed for the near defeat. In 1974 she was replaced as prime minister and withdrew to write her memoirs. Four years later, Meir died at the age of eighty.

Mann, Peggy. *Golda: The Life of Israel's Prime Minister.* New York: Coward, McCann & Geoghegan, 1971.

Meir, Golda. *A Land of Our Own: An Oral Biography.* Edited by Marie Syrkin. New York: Putnam, 1973.

Meir, Golda. *My Life.* New York: Putnam, 1975.

Meir, Menachem. *My Mother: Golda Meir.* New York: Arbor, 1983.

Simon Wiesenthal

1908-

Personal Background

Early life. Simon Wiesenthal was born December 31, 1908, the first son of Jewish parents living in the small town of Buczacs (now Lemberg in Ukraine, a southeast European republic that declared its independence in 1991 after the breakup of the Soviet Union). At the time, Eastern Europe was a hotbed of anti-Semitism (hostile discrimination against the Jewish people). In many places Jews faced housing and employment restrictions. Buczacs was a community with nine thousand residents, six thousand of whom were Jews. Many of these people had descended from farm families, but Jews who were subjects of the ruling Austro-Hungarian empire were prohibited from owning farms, so many had moved to towns and become craftsmen instead.

When World War I began, Wiesenthal's father was drafted into the Austrian army. He died in action, leaving his wife in Buczacs to care for the family. Conditions grew worse for Jews during the war, and for a time the Wiesenthal family was forced to take up residence in Vienna, Austria.

Back in Buczacs after World War I had ended, Simon enrolled in the Gymnasium, the European college preparatory school. He graduated in 1928 and applied for admission to the Technical University in Prague, Czechoslovakia. After four years

▲ Simon Wiesenthal

Event: Ensuring the memory of the Holocaust.

Role: Simon Wiesenthal lived through the horrors of European domination by the German Nazi party, witnessing the increasing violence of anti-Semitism before World War II and then surviving imprisonment in Nazi death camps. After the war, Wiesenthal dedicated his life to tracking down and bringing to justice the Nazis who had led the Holocaust—Adolf Hitler's drive to exterminate all European Jews.

he received his degree in architectural engineering, moved back to his hometown (by then called Lemberg), established an architectural firm specializing in home designs, and was an immediate success. In nearby Germany, however, events were changing the lives of European Jews forever.

Hitler's rise. In 1933 Nazi party leader Adolf Hitler was appointed chancellor of Germany and was on his way to becoming dictator of much of Europe. (The National Socialist, or Nazi, party was formed after Germany's defeat in World War I. Its members maintained strict nationalistic and racist ideals, opposed democracy, advocated world-wide expansion, and fed on hatred, prejudice, and violence.) To gain power, Hitler declared a death penalty for any offense against public security and appointed two strong Nazi officials to enforce his rules. Joseph Goebbels was named Minister for People's Enlightenment and Propaganda—without any restrictions about how he should "enlighten" the people. Heinrich Himmler was named head of the legal enforcers of Nazism: the SS (Schutzstaffel, or protective force) and the Gestapo (secret state police). Soon new laws banned Jews from working in civil service, medical, educational, legal, cultural, media, or entertainment-related occupations.

Two years later, during their annual meeting at Nuremberg, the Nazi party stepped up their persecutions of the Jews by establishing the Nuremberg Laws. Among other restrictions, Jews were barred from citizenship in the new Nazi Germany, and marriages between Jews and non-Jews became a national offense. Jews throughout Europe watched the actions of the Nazis with alarm.

Kristallnacht. Then, in 1938, European Jews were jolted with a sudden awakening to what the Nazi regime really planned for them. A German clerk in the Paris embassy was assassinated, and the Nazis used this as an excuse to accuse all Jews of plots against the government. SS troops stormed through Jewish communities, smashing storefronts, dragging Jews from their homes, beating them, and carting some off to prison. During the night raids of November 9 and 10, seven thousand Jewish businesses in

▲ Nazi youth bearing torches and swastika banners arrive at the University of Berlin grounds, where the Nazis burned about twenty thousand literary volumes that they deemed "contrary to the German spirit," 1933; in 1938 European Jews were jolted with a sudden awakening to what the Nazi regime really planned for them.

taken off to concentration camps. The siege that became known as Kristallnacht (because of all the broken glass) signaled Hitler's decision about the fate of European Jews. In Lemberg, the Wiesenthals watched in distant horror. The next year would bring the nightmare closer to reality.

Czechoslovakia and Poland. In 1939 the German army invaded Czechoslovakia and Poland. The occupation was swift and complete. Within two years, Germany had secured Poland and was prepared to march toward Russia. The German army easily overtook Lemberg and other towns in the area near the Polish border. By June 1941 the Germans had killed six thousand Jews and frightened the rest of the Jewish population into hiding or fleeing for their lives. On July 6, while hiding in his cellar, Simon Wiesenthal was arrested along with a friend and taken to prison. There Wiesenthal was sentenced to death for being a Jew, but several exceptionally lucky events postponed his execution:

> [The prisoners] were ordered to face the prison wall and put their hands behind their backs. Next to each man was a wooden crate—his coffin. A Ukrainian policeman started at one end of the wall and began shooting each prisoner in the back of the neck. In between shots, while the body was thrown into the crate, the Ukrainian drank vodka and ate sausage.

> Suddenly there was the familiar sound of the evening church bells. A guard called out that that was enough for one day, and that it was time to drink. (Wiesenthal 1979, p. 9)

Wiesenthal was not killed. Later, a guard he knew only by the name Bodnar offered to help him escape. (The guard had worked as a construction foreman on Wiesenthal-designed houses.) They staged a scuffle one night in which Wiesenthal and a friend were accused of being caught spying for the Russians. Both men were severely beaten and then led out of the prison by Bodnar on the excuse that they were to be interrogated. In this way, Wiesenthal made his first escape from the Nazis.

Sent to Janowska. A few weeks after Wiesenthal's escape, the Germans decided to make their work easier by herding all Jews into a designated section of town—a ghetto. It was easier then to select the young and healthy to be sent to forced labor camps, where they would make munitions and other war supplies. (During the war, Germany fueled its army by forcing war prisoners to work long hours with little food.) The confinement in the ghetto also made it easier for the SS troops to round up elderly Jews and kill them on the spot.

After returning to his home, Wiesenthal was arrested for a second time by the Nazis. He was young, so he was sent off first to a concentration camp at Janowska and then to work at the East-

▲ SS troops pass through Budapest in October 1941; Wiesenthal discovered that all of the survivors of the Nazi concentration camps distinctly remembered their torture at the hands of the SS troops.

ern Railroad Repair Works, painting swastikas (Nazi symbols shaped like angled crosses) on captured Soviet trains. On January 20, 1942, Hitler, Himmler, and SS Chief Reinhard Heydrich decided on the "final solution" to the Jewish "problem": all Jews in Europe would be rounded up and exterminated.

Saved once more. April 20, 1943 was a special day for the Nazis—Hitler's birthday. To celebrate, the Germans selected forty Jews laboring at the railroad works to be executed. Wiesenthal was among them. He and the others were to be led down a barbed-wire-lined column toward a sand pit where some dead bodies were already piled. They were ordered to remove their clothing and to begin to walk the path to death. Once again, Wiesenthal was saved by what might be called a miracle. His boss, a man named Kohlrautz, was secretly anti-Nazi and opposed the mistreatment of Jews. He told the SS officer in charge that

▲ **Wiesenthal tours the Jewish Historical Museum in Amsterdam, May 1987; it remains his personal mission to teach the lessons of Nazi hatred and brutality so that this bleak era in history will never be repeated.**

Wiesenthal's skill in painting was needed in order to finish the decorations for Hitler's birthday celebration that evening. Wiesenthal was spared.

Later Wiesenthal and a friend named Arthur Scheiman were given a pass to go into town to purchase more supplies. They made their escape through the back door of the store and were free for more than eight months.

Wiesenthal's capture. In June 1944 Wiesenthal was again arrested by the Gestapo. His previous escapes had been an embarrassment to the Nazis, so he thought that this time he would be subjected to the harshest of punishments. He first tried to escape his torturous fate with an unsuccessful suicide attempt. He was then shuffled in and out of several concentration camps. On February 7, 1945, nearly dead from his own wounds and the treatment at the camps, Wiesenthal was finally deposited at Mauthausen, a death camp in Austria. Too weak for the Germans to bother with, he was thrown into a hut and left to die. Wiesenthal had already shrunk to less than one hundred pounds.

Participation: Ensuring the Memory of the Holocaust

Nazi hunter. Three months later, Mauthausen concentration camp was liberated by American armored troops, and Wiesenthal was freed. He soon decided that his life would be dedicated to tracking down the war criminals who had put Hitler's "final solution" into action. He joined the War Crimes Division of the U.S. Army. Wiesenthal began his duties without formal training as an investigator but with a powerful urge to see justice done.

Later in 1945, Wiesenthal became head of the Jewish Central Committee in the zone of Austria that was, at that time, occupied by the United States. Those Jews who had survived the concentration camps needed help in restarting their lives and in locating their families. Wiesenthal's committee made careful lists of the camp survivors and those who were known to have died and tried to match them with relatives. In the process, he discovered that all of the ex-prisoners distinctly remembered their torture at the hands of the SS troops.

Nuremberg. The first Nazis accused of war crimes were tried in Nuremberg. Those found guilty were executed or imprisoned. The trials revealed far greater mistreatment of Jews and political prisoners than had ever been suspected. It was time for Wiesenthal to step up his activities. He had a long list of war criminals—names like Josef Mengele, Karl Babor, Franz Stangl, Kurt Wiese, Franz Murer, and Adolf Eichmann—and he devoted his life to pursuing them.

Franz Murer. Known as the "Butcher of Vilna," Franz Murer was responsible for killing approximately eighty thousand Lithuanian Jews who had been gathered together at Vilna in Estonia. Wiesenthal was searching for Adolf Eichmann when he discovered Murer. He gathered evidence against Murer from seven survivors of the Lithuanian extermination. Murer was arrested on his farm at Styria, Austria, and sent to the Soviet Union for trial. There a court found him guilty and sentenced him to twenty-five years in prison. A quirk of history, however, caused the Soviets to release Murer to Austria. In 1955 the Soviet Union—in connection with the Austria State Treaty—undertook to repatriate all prisoners of war (return them to their country of origin). Murer returned to his farm and became a respected member of the Austrian People's Party (Wiesenthal 1989, p 16).

But Wiesenthal succeeded in gaining a new trial for Murer, and he brought even more powerful testimony to the second hearing. Still, Murer was acquitted. Wiesenthal was not surprised by the verdict, but he was encouraged by the unexpected support of Roman Catholics, who staged protests and demonstrations over the outcome of the case. His actions were indeed having an effect on the public.

Adolf Eichmann. Wiesenthal's search for Adolf Eichmann, the man who had organized the concentration camps, finally ended when Israeli agents identified Eichmann living in Buenos Aires, Argentina, under the name Richardo Klament. Due to Wiesenthal's efforts, this elusive war criminal was brought to trial, found guilty of mass murders, and executed.

Anne Frank's memory. Wiesenthal also set out to perpetuate the memory of the Holocaust in all its vivid horror. Anne Frank was a young girl who hid with her family from the Nazis for two years before being discovered and arrested. They were sent to Auschwitz and then to Bergen-Belsen (both notorious concentration camps). Frank died of typhus in 1945 while still in prison. She had, however, kept a diary before her arrest, which her father

The Nazi Hunt

Wiesenthal has continued to bring Nazis to justice, persistently pursuing his foes and gathering evidence against them. Still, he is a champion of justice—not revenge. On occasions when Nazis or Nazi sympathizers have been brought to trial for crimes they did not commit, Wiesenthal has used his organizational skills to gather evidence for their acquittal. Such was the case of an SS officer named Beck; evidence revealed that Beck had actually treated Jewish camp prisoners in his charge as kindly as possible under the circumstances. In this case, Wiesenthal gathered additional evidence that won Beck's freedom.

later helped publish. It provided dramatic evidence of the reality of the Holocaust at a time in postwar history when the full magnitude of the Jewish massacre was not yet understood.

Wiesenthal set out to prove the validity of Frank's diary by locating the Gestapo agent who had arrested the Frank family. The search eventually led to Austria, a country that was uncooperative in war criminal investigations. Nevertheless, Wiesenthal was able to identify Karl Silberbauer as the Gestapo agent in the Frank case. The Austrians tried to suppress information about Silberbauer's past because he was working as an Austrian police inspector. Wiesenthal used the press to announce his findings. The diary of Anne Frank was proven true, and the reality of the Holocaust was supported by one more bit of evidence.

Aftermath

As of the mid-1990s, Wiesenthal continued to search for war criminals and strove to keep the horrors of the Holocaust fresh in the minds of new generations. Holocaust memorials and museums have been erected in his name. In all, eighty-nine members of Wiesenthal's family were exterminated at the hands of the Nazis. It remains his personal mission to teach the lessons of Nazi hatred and brutality so that this bleak era in history will never be repeated.

For More Information

Wiesenthal, Simon. *Nazi Hunter*. New York: Grove-Atlantic, 1979.
Wiesenthal, Simon. *Justice Not Vengeance*. New York: Grove-Atlantic, 1989.

Breakthroughs in Science and Technology

1928
▼
Alexander Fleming discovers penicillin.

1938
▼
Howard Florey begins his penicillin research.

1939
▼
William Shockley begins work on semiconductors.

1942
▼
Fleming supports therapeutic use of penicillin on British soldiers.

1945
▼
With the end of World War II, penicillin is brought into public use. Fleming, Florey, and Ernst Chain share the Nobel Prize for medicine.

1947
▼
Shockley helps to invent the transistor.

1951
▼
James Watson and Francis Crick discover the structure of DNA. **Rachel Carson** publishes *The Sea around Us.*

1956
▼
Shockley, John Bardeen, and Walter Brattain win the Nobel Prize for physics.

1959
▼
Computer chip is introduced, containing many transistors on a single silicon wafer.

1962
▼
Rachel Carson publishes *Silent Spring,* calling attention to the dangers of agricultural pesticides. Watson, Crick, and Maurice Wilkins share the Nobel Prize for medicine.

BREAKTHROUGHS IN SCIENCE AND TECHNOLOGY

Science is a study of the physical world that seeks to discover how and why things happen. Technology is an application of scientific methods to achieve a goal—the goal of overcoming the limits of nature to benefit humanity. Since the end of World War II in 1945, the scientific and technological struggle for advancement has become extremely powerful—with larger stakes than ever before. By the dawn of the twenty-first century, science and technology were bringing huge benefits to humanity, but not without equally huge risks.

During the twentieth century some fields of science and technology moved at revolutionary paces, with single great events directing the change. In the medical field, for instance, advances have been made that have saved or improved millions of human lives. At the same time, advancements in electronic technology have changed the way we live.

Antibiotics. Few events have had a wider impact in medicine than the discovery of antibiotics. In 1928 **Alexander Fleming,** a Scottish-born doctor working in London, observed a substance called penicillin that seemed to kill certain kinds of bacteria. It was one of science's most famous "accidents": a blue mold containing penicillin accidentally contaminated one of

Fleming's bacteria experiments—an experiment he was about to throw out. More than a decade later, other researchers, led by Howard Florey, finally demonstrated penicillin's bacteria-fighting capability. Called a "miracle cure" upon its discovery, penicillin first came into wide use near the end of World War II, when it was given to prevent and treat bacterial infections in wounded soldiers. Since then, many other antibiotics (bacteria-fighting agents such as penicillin) have been discovered.

DNA. Another revolutionary event in science occurred shortly after World War II. In 1951 **James Watson** and Francis Crick discovered the structure of DNA (deoxyribonucleic acid), the molecule in living cells that passes along genetic information. Working with Tinkertoy-like models, Watson and Crick determined that DNA is shaped like a spiral staircase, or "double helix." The secret of life itself is locked into the millions of links that form a single DNA chain.

Transistors. At about the same time, English-born American physicist **William Shockley** was leading the research team that invented and developed the transistor, an electronic device usually used for amplification or electric current conversion. Transistors replaced clunky vacuum tubes and opened up a new age in electronics and computers. Their invention brought rapid improvements in consumer electronics technology, making possible the development of state-of-the-art radios, television sets, and computers.

Environmental awareness. Scientific progress has spawned serious environmental concerns. One of the first instances of widespread public alarm about the state of the environment came from the dangers of the chemical pesticide DDT. Hailed as a miracle discovery in the 1950s for its ability to kill mosquitoes, lice, and fleas when sprayed into the environment, it sharply reduced the incidence of malaria, typhus, yellow fever, plague, and other diseases spread by these insects. DDT was being used by the ton across the United States for years, but one day in 1958 a Massachusetts woman named Olga Huckins found birds dropping dead from the trees after it was sprayed into the air over her rural town. Outraged and alarmed, Huckins wrote about her concerns to her friend, bestselling author **Rachel Carson.**

Carson was a trained biologist whose poetically written books about the sea made her a nationally renowned literary figure. Her research into DDT was published as *Silent Spring* in 1962 and created a massive public outcry. Carson showed in compelling detail the dangers that commonly used poisons like DDT—which are passed along the food chain—pose to human, animal, and plant life. This single book is credited with having started the environmental movement. It also led to the passage of early environmental laws.

Advancement at what cost? Although we derive clear benefits from scientific and technological advances like penicillin and transistors, many scientists warn that we must guard our place in the world, making the fewest possible changes to nature to achieve our goals. The greater the impact of our actions, they conclude, the greater the risk to our own well-being.

Alexander Fleming

1881-1955

Personal Background

Alexander Fleming was born on August 6, 1881, on his family's sheep farm in southwestern Scotland, near the town of Darvel. He was the seventh of eight children, and his father, Hugh Fleming, was in his sixties when Alexander was born. Hugh Fleming had been married once before, but his first wife had died. Four of Alexander's older brothers and sisters were born of this first marriage, and two were from his father's second marriage—to Grace Morton, Alexander's mother.

Scrapes. Alexander was followed two years later by a younger brother, Robert, his companion throughout childhood. Alec, as he was called, loved practical jokes and games of all kinds. A highly competitive youngster, he was always getting into scrapes of one kind or another. Once, when tearing around a corner, he apparently ran smack into another boy, whose head hit him right on the nose. Fleming's nose, it later turned out, was badly broken. After that, it would always have a pushed-in appearance, leading to rumors that penicillin's discoverer had been a well-known boxer.

London. In 1895, at the age of fourteen, Alec quit school and moved to London, far to the south in England. There his older brothers Tom and John and sister Mary had set up house together. Soon after, Robert moved in, too. The boys adjusted well

▲ **Alexander Fleming**

Event: The discovery of penicillin.

Role: In 1928 Scottish-born scientist Alexander Fleming discovered bacteria-killing mold growing on culture plates. He identified the ingredient in the mold that had killed the bacteria, naming it penicillin. It soon became known as the "miracle cure" for infections.

to city life, enjoying the bustle and all the new sights. Alec landed a job as a shipping clerk, and he and Robert joined the army reserve in 1900, serving in the London Scottish Rifle Volunteers. By the time he was twenty, however, he began to regret leaving school, where he had always done well. He didn't want to be a shipping clerk for the rest of his life. Tom, a doctor, suggested Alec enroll in medical school, so in 1901 he took the entrance exam. Though he had been out of school for over five years, he tied for the highest score on the test.

Bacteria and Inoculation

Though most bacteria are harmless or even helpful to humans, some can cause deadly diseases and infections. When Fleming began his studies, bacterial illness killed millions of people every year. Bacterial research was in its infancy, led by scientists like Louis Pasteur of France. Sir Almroth Wright believed in the power of vaccines (or inoculations), which Pasteur had developed as a way of fighting disease.

Inoculation works by introducing a weakened form of a certain disease into the body through a shot. This weak form, called a vaccine, helps the body's immune system create defenses against the stronger form.

St. Mary's. That October, Fleming enrolled at St. Mary's Hospital Medical School, which he chose because it was close to the house he shared with his brothers and sister. At that time, London had twelve teaching hospitals that trained most doctors. Some dated as far back as the twelfth century, but St. Mary's was the newest, having been founded in 1845. Each of these private institutions had its own character, and each inspired great loyalty among its members. In fact, Alexander Fleming remained at St. Mary's for his entire working life—over half a century.

Participation: The Discovery of Penicillin

Fleming was a naturally gifted student. In his first few years of medical study at St. Mary's, he won many of the school's yearly prizes in subjects like chemistry, biology, and anatomy. In some ways, he viewed it all as just another of his endless games. A friend of his who often came in second to him complained that he had to work harder for second place than Fleming did for first.

Sir Almroth Wright. In 1904 Fleming and his classmates moved on to their clinical studies, working with patients under the guidance of experienced doctors in the hospital. Many of the patients suffered from bacterial infections that caused great discomfort and often proved fatal.

The study of bacteria is called bacteriology, and one of Britain's leading bacteriologists happened to work at St. Mary's. His name was Almroth Wright, and he had taken up a crusade against the deadly effects of bacteria. At this point in time, Fleming had no firm plans for the future, though he was beginning to take an interest in becoming a surgeon. (Surgeons commanded the most respect in the medical world.) In 1906, after Fleming finished his clinical work and final exams, Wright offered him a job in the hospital's inoculation department. Fleming took the job, thinking he would eventually move on to be a surgeon. Soon, however, he was an enthusiastic fighter in Wright's battle against bacteria.

Contrasting Figures

Fleming became one of Wright's many followers, although the two could not have been more different in appearance. Wright was a huge bear of a man, while Fleming was small—about five-feet five-inches tall—though wiry and athletic. They also differed in their approaches to life: Wright's seriousness was equaled by Fleming's playfulness (though Fleming, uncomfortable with small talk, is said to have puzzled people with frequent, long silences in conversation).

World War I. In 1914, when World War I broke out, the war against bacteria entered a new stage. Vaccines were proven effective in preventing many bacterial illnesses. Wright offered the services of his whole department to the British government for use in inoculating troops. He believed they could prevent the infections that often killed the wounded. Wright, Fleming, and some others in the department spent the war years in France, where they worked on new ways of saving the lives of soldiers exposed to disease in unhealthy battlefield conditions.

Lysozyme. In 1921, having returned to England after the war's end, Fleming thought he had found something. He was cleaning up his lab, which was always cluttered with the dishes used to grow bacteria. On one of the old dishes, he had been growing bacteria from mucus from his own nose. He noticed that outside bacteria had gotten in and started growing in the dish—except in the area right around the mucus. Somehow the mucus prevented its growth. Fleming began experimenting with other people's mucus, and then with other body fluids, such as tears and saliva. He found that these fluids naturally contain a mild antiseptic of their own, which came to be called lysozyme.

In further experiments, however, Fleming found that lysozyme killed mostly harmless bacteria. It was not very effective against bacteria linked to diseases or infections. (It is now known to be part of the body's early defense against common bacteria.) Disappointed, by 1926 Fleming had moved on to other research.

A funny blue mold. Two years later Fleming once again noticed something in an old dish that he was about to clean up. He had just returned from vacation and was stacking old dishes in a tub of disinfectant to get them ready for new experiments. Something drew his attention to a dish at the top of the stack. "That's funny," he is said to have remarked to a coworker (Fleming in Macfarlane, p. 119). It was the same situation that had led to his discovery of lysozyme, but instead of mucus it was a bit of blue mold growing in the old dish that had cleared the area around it of bacteria. This time, however, the bacteria was a type that could cause serious infections—and something in the mold had killed it.

The discovery of penicillin. Fleming began a series of experiments to determine how the mold had killed the bacteria. Having discovered that the mold was a kind known as *penicillium* (commonly found on rotting fruit or bread), he named its antibacterial ingredient penicillin. Despite his early hopes, however, penicillin proved very hard to work with. It was extremely difficult to separate the bacteria-fighting agent from the mold, and large quantities of mold were needed to make even a small amount of penicillin. Furthermore, penicillin lost its strength quickly—usually within a half hour.

Fleming assigned some of his assistants the job of improving penicillin. When he tested it on a patient with an eye infection, the infection went away quickly. In this case, he applied it directly, using an eye dropper. When injected into healthy lab animals, it proved harmless. But Fleming did not test the effects of penicillin injections in sick animals. After about six months of experiments, he lost most of his interest in its medicinal properties.

Howard Florey. Fleming had married in 1915, just after the outbreak of World War I. He and his wife, Sarah, had a baby boy,

Robert, in 1924. Despite his disappointments with lysozyme and penicillin, the 1920s and 1930s were happy years for Alexander Fleming and his family.

In 1938, ten years after Fleming discovered penicillin, another scientist began experimenting with it in Oxford, about an hour's train ride outside of London. (The Flemings maintained an apartment in London and a house in the English countryside.) Howard Florey, an Australian doctor working at Oxford University, had been in touch with Fleming about lysozyme. With Ernst Chain, a Jewish scientist who had fled the wartime dangers during Adolf Hitler's rise in Nazi Germany, Florey had succeeded in making a pure form of lysozyme. (Lysozyme was shown to be an enzyme—or protein molecule that causes chemical reactions—found in human tears and saliva.) Florey then read a 1929 paper by Fleming about penicillin and became interested in studying its bacteria-fighting characteristics.

By early 1940, Florey, Chain, and others working with them succeeded in making a much stronger and purer form of penicillin. Then they took the simple step that Fleming had failed to take: they tested it by injecting it into sick animals, repeating the injections to make up for penicillin's loss of strength over time. At the end of one of their overnight tests, animals that should have been dead were in perfect health.

Fleming Improves the Treatment of Wounds

Fleming discovered that the antiseptic used to kill bacteria in wounds was also killing off the white blood cells that the body used to attack the bacteria. Deep in the wounds, the bacteria were escaping the antiseptics and continuing the infections. Therefore, Fleming and Wright advised doctors to rinse wounds not with strong antiseptics but with a special salt-water solution that would leave the white blood cells free to do their bacteria-fighting work.

"Miracle cure." Florey and his coworkers then had to perfect the vaccine for use in humans. It was a long, slow process. Tests on six seriously ill patients in early 1941 yielded encouraging results—only two deaths, one of which was not related to the use of the drug. But because Great Britain was now immersed in the darkest days of World War II, money for scientific research was scarce.

In August 1942 Fleming asked Florey for some penicillin to treat a seemingly hopeless patient in London. The patient made a

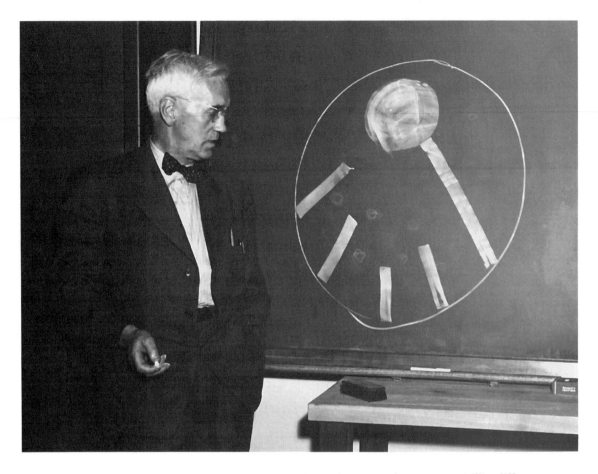

▲ Fleming demonstrating how the "miracle cure" penicillin diffuses, a property, he noted, that "makes it effective and superior to other antibiotics."

spectacular recovery—and Fleming's interest in penicillin was rekindled. He began pushing powerful friends in London to support penicillin production. As production increased, the army began using the drug on wounded soldiers. Reports spread of the "miracle cure" that put soldiers near death back on their feet in weeks or even days.

Aftermath

World fame. With such miraculous results, British and American drug companies and government agencies put great efforts into research on the improvement of penicillin production.

Soon new methods were developed for making stronger and purer forms of the antibiotic, and by the end of World War II penicillin had saved millions of lives.

After the war, reporters grew interested in the story behind the miracle cure. Howard Florey refused to be interviewed, but Fleming (losing his old quietness) enjoyed telling the dramatic tale of the blue mold that he had found by accident so long before. Public attention focused on Fleming, who received a hero's welcome everywhere he went. By contrast, newspaper stories almost always ignored Florey, Chain, and the others who worked with them in Oxford. This situation led to inevitable bitterness on their part.

Nobel Prize. Fleming and Florey were both knighted (given a title of honor and thereafter referred to as "Sir"), and with Chain they shared the Nobel Prize for medicine in 1945. Despite such shared honors, however, Alexander Fleming remains the most recognizable name in the discovery and refinement of penicillin. Fleming, youthful and energetic in his old age, remarried after his first wife's death in 1949. He died suddenly of a heart attack on March 11, 1955.

Antibiotics

People have used mold and similar organisms to treat infections for over three thousand years. Only in the late nineteenth century, when doctors first began to understand bacteria, did they begin to investigate the power of these natural bacteria killers. By the close of the twentieth century, many antibiotics had been found, though penicillin remained the most widely used. Researchers continue their search for new drugs because some bacteria seem to mutate, or change, and become resistant to certain antibiotics over time.

For More Information

Kaye, Judith. *The Life of Alexander Fleming*. New York: Holt, 1993.

Macfarlane, Gwyn. *Alexander Fleming: The Man and the Myth*. Cambridge, Massachusetts: Harvard University Press, 1984.

Otfinoski, Steven. *Alexander Fleming: Conquering Disease with Penicillin*. New York: Facts on File, 1992.

William Shockley

1910-1989

Personal Background

Birth. William Bradford Shockley was born on February 13, 1910, in London, England, to American parents. His father, William Hillman Shockley, worked in England as a mining engineer; his mother, May Bradford Shockley, was a mineral surveyor, someone who tells miners what minerals they can expect to find in a given area. Mining was very much a "man's job," especially in those days, but May Shockley was an unusual woman for her time. She had worked as a surveyor for the U.S. government during the Nevada gold rush in the late nineteenth century. Both of William's parents were highly intelligent, strong-willed people who challenged convention and societal trends.

Home education. The Shockleys moved back home to Palo Alto, California, when William was three. William received his earliest education at home. When he began attending school, both his parents continued to coach him—his father in science and his mother in mathematics. And one of their neighbors, a professor of physics, sparked Shockley's early curiosity in that field. In 1932 he earned his undergraduate degree in physics from the California Institute of Technology in Pasadena.

Participation: The Invention of the Transistor

Crystals. After graduating, Shockley won a teaching fellow-

▲ **William Shockley**

Event: The invention of the transistor.

Role: A prize-winning American physicist, William Shockley led the team of scientists who, in 1947, invented one of the most important electrical devices of the modern age: the transistor.

ship at the Massachusetts Institute of Technology, where he also began his graduate work. His doctoral thesis examined the behavior of electrons in crystals, part of a study area called "solid-state" physics. Solid-state physics deals with how solids—metals or rubber, for example—interact with electricity. Shockley finished his thesis and earned his doctoral degree in 1936.

Bell Labs. Turning down offers from General Electric and Yale University, Shockley took a job at the Bell Telephone Laboratories in Murray Hill, New Jersey. For several years, he worked on vacuum tubes, light-bulb-sized devices that were then the basic part of any electronic instrument. The Bell Telephone Company wished to improve its switchboards so that phone connections could be made by electronic switches instead of by mechanical ones. As more people began using phones, the old mechanical switchboards became overloaded. Bell researchers hoped to make a vacuum tube that could do the job of switching calls quickly and efficiently.

Vacuum tubes, like light bulbs, heated up as electric current passed through them. This signaled a lack of efficiency. (Heat is actually wasted energy.) In addition, vacuum tubes burned out quickly, making them expensive to operate on a large scale. So Shockley began thinking about other ways of handling electrical currents. By 1939 he was focusing on materials called semiconductors. As the name indicates, these are substances whose ability to carry electrical current is lower than that of conductors (like metals) and higher than that of insulators (like rubber).

Operations research. Shockley's research was interrupted by World War II. He went to work for the U.S. government for five years, from 1940 to 1945. Most of that time he spent doing "operations research" on antisubmarine warfare—figuring out how well the military's weapons were performing.

Semiconductors. After the war, Shockley returned to Bell Labs and resumed his work on semiconductors. He was put in charge of a team of researchers that included Walter Brattain and John Bardeen. Brattain's specialty was setting up experiments, while Bardeen's job was to interpret the results of the experiments. Shockley oversaw the research team.

Semiconductors are basically bits of silicon or related material, similar to a grain of sand in chemical makeup. Shockley believed that such material could be used as a switch—that its conducting ability could be controlled to change the flow and direction of an electrical current. He was also convinced that it could act as an amplifier, allowing a weak current to be made much stronger. Switching and amplifying an electrical current were, until this time, only accomplished with vacuum tubes. Shockley's vision of a semiconducting amplifier and switch guided him as the team leader.

Field effect leads to transistor breakthrough. Shockley theorized that a semiconductor's conducting ability might be easily controlled by changing the electrical field around it. But it was difficult to make this "field effect" work in experiments. Bardeen suggested that an unknown surface interference might function to stop the current.

The team tried getting around the surface interference by inserting two tiny wires, or contact points, and a metal plate very close together on the surface of a semiconducting material. They discovered that a weak current sent through one wire would reach a metal plate on the other side, opening up a "hole" for a much stronger current to pass through from the second wire. The hole could be made larger or smaller by changing the first current, depending on the desired strength of the second current. The structure was like a sandwich, with the wires and the metal plate as the bread, and the semiconducting material as the filling. This sandwich arrangement broke the surface interference, creating the switch and amplifier they were looking for, with the weak current acting as a valve for the strong one. The key was in controlling the weak current: small changes in it could cause large changes in the strong current.

Improvements. Most of these discoveries were made in December 1947 and announced in a press conference in June of the following year. But when Shockley determined that the tran-

> ### How the Transistor Got Its Name
>
> At the time of its discovery, just how the weak current opened up the mysterious "hole" for an electric current was not clearly understood. Shockley, Brattain, and Bardeen called the process "transfer of resistance" and named their device a "transfer resistor." It was one of their fellow Bell scientists, John R. Pierce, who shortened this to "transistor."

sistor's wire contact points could easily be broken or dislodged, he immediately began work on an improved version. Within a month, he had come up with a new design, replacing the early "point contact" transistor with the more rugged "junction" transistor. This design took two years to perfect, and it was 1951 before it began appearing in consumer items such as radios, microphones, and hearing aids. The junction transistor quickly became the backbone of the electronics industry. In 1956 Shockley, Brattain, and Bardeen won the Nobel Prize for physics for their invention.

Computer chip. The junction transistor was the ancestor of the computer chip, first developed in 1959, which packs many transistors into a single, tiny silicon wafer. By the mid-1990s one of these fingernail-sized slivers could hold millions of transistors. Shockley's transistor sparked the computer revolution.

Aftermath

Going into business. In 1954 Shockley left Bell Labs to take advantage of the business opportunities his invention offered. He, his wife, and three children returned to California, settling in Palo Alto, where Shockley had lived as a child. There he set up Shockley Semiconductor Laboratories, which he later sold for a large profit. As the computer revolution gathered speed, other electronics companies followed Shockley to this area of California, giving it the nickname "Silicon Valley." After selling his company in the early 1960s, Shockley became a professor at nearby Stanford University, where he taught electrical engineering until his retirement in the 1970s.

Racial theories of intelligence. In the late 1960s and early 1970s, Shockley caused considerable controversy in a very different area—the field of social science. He had studied the results of intelligence

Tubes Versus Chips

When Shockley invented the transistor, the computer industry had reached a dead end. Computers used up so many bulky vacuum tubes that several rooms were needed to house them. And the expensive tubes burned out so fast that in large computers simply replacing them was a full-time job. On top of that, each one required about a full watt of power. Today's microchips, based on transistor technology, are millions of times smaller, cheaper, longer-lasting, and more efficient.

tests and concluded that intelligence is related to race. Shockley's theory centered on the idea that intelligence is passed on genetically and that whites naturally possess a higher degree of intelligence than nonwhites.

During the civil rights movement of the 1960s, when African Americans were in the thick of their long struggle for equality, Shockley's statements stirred up social unrest. His discriminatory views tarnished his reputation in the scientific community. Students at Stanford protested in his classes and publicly burned a Shockley dummy on campus. Articles and talk shows featured interviews with him and with those who opposed his racist ideas. Many interviewers were outraged by his statements and questioned his motivations; soon he and his wife were recording all of their daily conversations with others (using, of course, transistorized tape recorders).

William Shockley died on August 12, 1989, having cast a huge shadow on race relations, while leaving an enormous legacy in scientific advancement.

For More Information

Aaseng, Nathan. *The Inventors: Nobel Prizes in Chemistry, Physics and Medicine.* Minneapolis: Lerner, 1988.

Aaseng, Nathan. *Twentieth-Century Inventors.* New York: Facts on File, 1991.

Boeth, Richard. "The Great IQ Controversy." *Newsweek,* December 17, 1973, p. 109.

Rogers, Michael. "Brave New William Shockley." *Esquire,* January 1973, p. 130.

Thomas, Shirley. *Men of Space.* Vol 4. Philadelphia and New York: Chilton, 1962.

Rachel Carson

1907-1964

Personal Background

Beginnings. Rachel Louise Carson was born on May 27, 1907, in Springdale, Pennsylvania, a small town in the Allegheny River Valley not far from Pittsburgh. The Carsons had settled on sixty-five acres of land in the countryside near Springdale. Rachel's father, Robert Carson, was a businessman who also kept a ten-acre apple orchard on the property.

Words and wonder. The strongest influence on Rachel during her childhood years was her mother, Maria Maclean Carson. A former schoolteacher who loved books, nature, and music, Maria Carson passed her quiet enthusiasm for learning to all of her children—but especially to Rachel. Despite frequent illnesses, Rachel usually spent her preschool days outdoors watching birds and other animals. She passed evenings with her family, singing at the piano or listening to her mother read stories out loud. Rachel learned to read at a very early age. She never lost her girlhood wonder about nature and its surprises, or her love of words and their strange power to build pictures in the mind.

First stories. When she was ten years old, Rachel Carson began writing stories, which her mother suggested she send in to a children's magazine. The magazine, *St. Nicholas,* was popular and widely read, and many famous writers had their first stories published in it. Over the next few years, Carson wrote several sto-

▲ Rachel Carson

Event: Birth of the environmental movement.

Role: Scientist and writer Rachel Carson introduced many readers to the sea and its creatures with her best-selling books. Her wide following and strong reputation helped set the stage for her last and most influential book, *Silent Spring,* in which she called attention to the dangers of pesticides and other synthetic chemicals. The book created a public outcry that led to early antipollution laws.

ries for *St. Nicholas*—she wanted to be a writer, a desire that stayed with her throughout high school. Carson became fascinated with the sea, though she had never even seen it, and wrote stories set on ships or on rugged, stormswept coastlines.

In 1925 Carson won a scholarship to attend the Pennsylvania College for Women (now Chatham College). There, majoring in literature, she wrote for college publications. During her junior year, however, she had to fulfill her science class requirements and signed up for biology. Carson became friends with her teacher, Mary Skinker, and soon found herself changing her major from literature to biology.

Woods Hole and Johns Hopkins. Though she loved writing, Carson never regretted her decision. She took a wide variety of science courses, but her studies focused on marine biology, the study of life in the sea. Graduating from college in 1929, she was awarded a fellowship for summer study at the Woods Hole Marine Biological Laboratory on Cape Cod. Her trip to the famous research center took her from New York harbor by boat. It was her first sight of the sea. Carson spent the entire summer studying at Woods Hole, working in the lab, and taking long walks along the shore. She would never again spend long periods of time away from the sea.

In the fall of 1929 Carson began her first year of graduate study at Johns Hopkins University in Baltimore, Maryland. Three years later, she obtained her master's degree in zoology. Meanwhile, her parents joined her in Maryland, and they lived together near Baltimore. The Great Depression (a severe economic crisis with high levels of unemployment brought on by the collapse of the U.S. stock market in 1929) had struck, and times were tough financially. Carson's brother, Robert, had lost his job and joined the household. Everyone had to pull together. For Carson, though, it was a time of learning and discovery.

"Fish Tales." The family was saddened by the death of Carson's father in 1935 and Rachel's older sister, Marian, in 1937. The year her father died, Carson landed a job as a writer for the Bureau of Fisheries in Washington, D.C. Elmer Higgins, the man who hired her, was looking for a scientist who could also write well. Carson worked on a series titled *Romance under the Waters,* though Higgins and his staff jokingly called it "Seven-Minute Fish Tales." Her job was to provide brief and interesting introductions to radio stories of life under the sea. When she turned in her first written introduction for approval, Higgins rejected it—because it was too good. He told her to write another introduction for radio and advised her to have the first one published in a literary magazine.

In 1937 the *Atlantic Monthly* published it as "Undersea." By now Carson had decided what she wanted to do: she wanted to inspire the average reader with her sensitive and artistic literary portraits of nature.

Participation:
Birth of the Environmental Movement

Under the Sea-Wind. "Undersea" received a favorable response from the *Atlantic*'s readers. Author Hendrik Willem Van Loon, who had penned a widely read book titled *The Story of Mankind,* was especially moved by Carson's work. He wrote to her, and she wrote back, telling him that she dreamed of writing a whole book about creatures who live in the sea. With Van Loon's encouragement, she began to put together an outline for the book and a first chapter. Van Loon's publisher, Simon & Schuster, was interested and gave her a $250 advance, but they would not sign a contract to publish the book until they had seen more chapters.

Working weekends and in the evenings after her full day at the Bureau of Fisheries, she had five chapters done by early 1940. Carson signed a contract and received another check. She began working faster. Her mother typed up the chapters as she finished writing

Scomber, A Young Mackerel

"In the surface waters Scomber first knew the fear of the hunted. On the tenth morning of his life he had lingered in the upper fathoms of water instead of following down into the soft gloom below. Out of the clear green water a dozen gleaming silver fishes suddenly loomed up. They were anchovies, small and herringlike. The foremost anchovy caught sight of Scomber. Swerving from his path, he came whirling through the yard of water that separated them, ready to seize the small mackerel. Scomber veered away in sudden alarm." (Carson from *Under the Sea-Wind,* pp. 131-32) them, and the following year her book was published. She gave it the title *Under the Sea-Wind.*

War years in Washington. Carson's book received excellent reviews and sold well at first, but just a few weeks after it came out the Japanese attacked Pearl Harbor and the United States entered World War II. People stopped buying books, and *Under the Sea-Wind* was forgotten as the country plunged into war. U.S. president Franklin Delano Roosevelt expanded the government during the war and made the Bureau of Fisheries part of the new U.S. Fish and Wildlife Service. Carson was made the service's editor in chief, overseeing all of its many publications. Her job and its responsibilities kept her busy during the early to mid-1940s.

Conservation. After the war, Carson worked on a series of pamphlets called *Conservation in Action.* In the introduction, she wrote:

> Wild creatures, like men, must have a place to live. As civilization creates cities, builds highways, and drains marshes, it takes away, little by little, the land that is suitable for wildlife. As their spaces for living dwindle, the wildlife populations themselves decline. (Carson in Goldberg, pp. 33-34)

Such ideas had been expressed earlier by writers like nineteenth-century American essayist Henry David Thoreau and Sierra Club founder John Muir. These conservationists (people who strive to protect and preserve the earth's resources for the future) objected to human settlement that threatened wildlife. As a naturalist, Carson felt strong sympathy for such views.

The Sea around Us. There was one book Carson herself wanted to read—but no one had written it. So she began work on it in 1948. Her goal was to describe not just sea life but also its environment—the whole sea itself—and its history. It was a huge job. As part of her research, she went diving in Florida and spent a week aboard the *Albatross III,* the Fish and Wildlife Service's seagoing research ship. Such ships had helped in the rapid progress of oceanography since the war's end in 1945. Carson's aim was to educate the general public about the oceans. In 1949 she won a $2,250 award, the Eugene F. Saxton Memorial, which allowed her to take a leave of absence from her job. She finished the book in 1950, and it was published the following year under the title *The Sea around Us.*

Bestsellers. Even before *The Sea around Us* came out, parts of it appeared in magazines such as the *Yale Review, Vogue,* and the *New Yorker.* Still, Carson and her publisher, Oxford University Press, were surprised by the book's success. It was an instant bestseller, staying on the *New York Times* bestseller list for almost two years. Carson was given honorary degrees from several universities, and *Under the Sea-Wind,* her forgotten first book, was republished. In 1952 it too made the bestseller list. Rachel Carson was by this time a famous American writer.

A new life. Carson could now afford to write full time, so she quit her job with the Fish and Wildlife Service, bought some land on the coast of Maine near the town of West Southport, and built a summer cottage there. Each summer for the rest of her life she would go to her cottage, passing her days writing and taking long walks along the shore. She usually took a canvas bag slung over her shoulder to collect interesting plants and animals from among the rocks and tide pools. In 1955 Carson's third book, *The Edge of the Sea,* came out. It was about the rugged creatures who live in the shoreline world she had been exploring, where sea meets land. It too became a bestseller.

Two years later, Carson's niece Marjorie died, and Carson adopted Marjorie's five-year-old son, Roger. Carson also looked after her mother, now almost ninety. It became hard sometimes to find the time and energy to write, but she worked on planning her next book—this one about the continents and their history.

"The tortured earth." In early 1958, however, Carson received a letter from her friend Olga Huckins, a journalist and fellow birdwatcher who lived in Duxbury, Massachusetts. Huckins told her about the spraying of her town by a "mosquito control plane" (Sterling, p. 147). After the plane's load of DDT, a commonly used pesticide, had settled over the town, birds literally began dropping dead from the trees. Huckins was outraged. "For those of us who stand helplessly on the tortured earth," Huckins wrote, "it is intolerable" (Huckins in Sterling, p. 148).

Silent Spring. For some time, Carson had known that pollution from waste—along with radiation from atomic bomb tests—caused damage to the environment. She had seen reports about how deadly poisons in pesticides were damaging wild animals and their environments. By the late 1950s these chemicals were being used widely around the world, especially in the United States. Pesticides effectively killed insects that carried disease and ate valuable crops, but their long-term effects on nature, wildlife, and humans had not been determined.

From *Silent Spring*

"For the first time in the history of the world, every human being is now subjected to contact with dangerous chemicals, from the moment of conception until death. In the less than two decades of their use [as of 1962], the synthetic pesticides have been so thoroughly distributed ... that they occur virtually everywhere. They have entered and lodged in the bodies of fish, birds, reptiles, and domestic and wild animals so universally that scientists carrying on animal experiments find it almost impossible to locate subjects free from such contamination." (pp. 15-16)

Focusing on pesticides, and DDT in particular, Carson began working on a new book. Around the same time, she was told she had breast cancer. An operation and the anticancer treatments that followed made her feel sick and exhausted. But in 1962 the first parts of her book were excerpted in the *New Yorker.* Other magazines had refused to publish them, for fear of losing the advertising of powerful chemical companies that made the pesticides. Later that year, the complete book was published under the title *Silent Spring.*

"Since Miss Carson's book." In *Silent Spring,* Carson revealed that DDT had dangerous effects that chemical companies and the government had hidden from the public. She showed how such pesticides washed into rivers and lakes from the soil, killed fish, built up in the bodies of wild animals—and thus entered the food chain itself. Humans who consumed the contaminated water, vegetables, fish, and meat were threatened. Carson viewed the widespread use of these poisons as an unacceptable risk to all living things.

Silent Spring created a public outcry. In response, food and chemical companies attacked Carson and her ideas, portraying her as a nutty old lady who was obsessed over a few dead birds. Yet her solid facts, backed up by careful research, could not be ignored. Politicians around the country became concerned with the environment for the first time. At a press conference, a reporter asked President John F. Kennedy whether the U.S. government was going to think about controlling the use of pesticides. "Yes," Kennedy answered, "and I know they already are. I think, particularly, since Miss Carson's book" (Kennedy in Sterling, p. 169).

Aftermath

Much else has happened "since Miss Carson's book," as environmental issues have taken a central place in public life. Rachel Carson, however, did not live to see these developments. After calmly defending her work in interviews and after winning many more awards and honors, she died of cancer on April 14, 1964, at the age of fifty-six.

For More Information

Carson, Rachel. *Under the Sea-Wind*. Originally published in 1941. Fiftieth anniversary ed. New York: Dutton, 1991.

Carson, Rachel. *The Sea around Us*. New York: Oxford University Press, 1951.

Carson, Rachel. *Silent Spring*. Originally published in 1962. Twenty-fifth anniversary ed. New York: Houghton, 1987.

Goldberg, Jake. *Rachel Carson*. Broomall, Pennsylvania: Chelsea House, 1992.

Henrickson, John. *Rachel Carson*. Brookfield, Connecticut: Millbrook, 1991.

Sterling, Philip. *Sea and Earth: The Life of Rachel Carson*. New York: Crowell, 1970.

James Watson

1928-

Personal Background

Early signs. James Dewey Watson was the leading American geneticist of his era. (A geneticist is a biologist who studies the science of heredity, or characteristics that are passed from parent to offspring.) He was born on April 6, 1928, in Chicago, Illinois, where he and his younger sister, Elizabeth, grew up and went to school. Considered a "child prodigy," he possessed intellectual abilities that exceeded those of adults.

Birds and genetics. Watson's unusual powers of memory led to his success as a radio "quiz kid" in the 1930s and 1940s. Completing high school in two years, he enrolled at the University of Chicago when he was just fifteen years old. He loved bird-watching and thought about majoring in ornithology, the study of birds. Ultimately, however, he studied biology. Four years later, near the age when other young men and women were beginning college, Watson graduated. He had developed a keen interest in genetics while attending the University of Chicago, and in 1947 he enrolled at the University of Indiana to pursue graduate study in that subject.

DNA. The University of Indiana was well known for its genetics program, which was headed by Nobel Prize-winning geneticist Hermann Müller and Italian microbiologist Salvador Luria. Watson arrived in 1947, just a few years after three scien-

▲ **James Watson**

Event: Discovery of the structure of DNA.

Role: A long, stringlike molecule hidden in the nucleus of living cells, DNA was shown in 1944 to be responsible for passing along genetic information in living things. In 1951 American biologist James Watson teamed up with British physicist Francis Crick to unravel the secret of DNA's structure. They won the Nobel Prize for their work in 1962.

tists, led by Oswald Avery, had uncovered evidence that DNA played a role in the passage of genetic instructions. At the time, their discovery was still not accepted by many scientists, but Watson was fascinated with the idea. Studying under Luria, he wrote his doctoral thesis on viruses, which multiply by building their own DNA from materials in the cells of other organisms.

Having earned his doctorate (Ph.D.) in 1950, Watson went to the University of Copenhagen in Denmark to study chemistry. The next year, he met an English scientist named Maurice Wilkins, who was using X rays to try to photograph DNA molecules. This sparked Watson's commitment to discovering the structure of DNA.

Participation:
Discovery of the Structure of DNA

Francis Crick. From Copenhagen, Watson managed to arrange a year of study in Cambridge, England, home of Cambridge University and its famous Cavendish Laboratory. Scientists there were working on the same sort of X-ray photography that Wilkins had told Watson about. One such scientist was British biophysicist Francis Crick, who was studying protein structure. Known for his talkative, fun-loving nature and big booming laugh, Crick made some of his colleagues nervous. He had a habit of poking his nose into their research and then coming up with answers to questions that they should have figured out for themselves.

Pauling's models. Meanwhile, American chemist Linus Pauling was constructing models of various molecules he was investigating. A brilliant scientist, Pauling used the rules of chemistry to fit together "Tinkertoy" pieces that stood for the atoms known to be present in a given molecule. Just before Watson

Genes

Genetics is the study of genes, the units of heredity in living organisms that pass along information from one generation to another. Genes are present in the nucleus of every cell of the human body (except red blood cells, which have no nucleus), and they determine such things as hair, eye, and skin color. In 1944 scientists showed that the information in genes is passed along by DNA (short for deoxyribonucleic acid). DNA gives cells "orders" about how to grow.

▲ **Working with Tinkertoy-like models, Watson and Francis Crick determined that DNA is shaped like a spiral staircase, or "double helix."**

arrived in Cambridge, Pauling had used his models to figure out the structure of a mysterious protein called the alpha-helix. (Pauling's model had shown that its shape was that of a helix, or coil.)

Watson was excited by the possibilities such models offered for understanding the structure of molecules. Unlike most British scientists, who saw the models as nearly useless toys, Crick too found the models helpful for visualizing molecular structure. Watson noted in his book *The Double Helix* that within a few days of meeting each other, he and Crick decided to use models in their attack on DNA's structure. They planned to "imitate Linus Pauling and beat him at his own game" (Watson, p. 32).

Using a process called X-ray crystallography, Watson and Crick took pictures of crystallized forms of DNA. The fact that DNA could be made into crystals—simple, orderly arrangements of atoms—suggested that its structure was based on a simple pattern. Watson soon discovered that proteins were closely linked to DNA; strands of DNA carried the information that built proteins, which were then used in making new cells as an organism grew. So the first pattern that Watson and Crick looked for was a helix—the coiled structure that Pauling had shown were associated with proteins.

In the fall of 1951, after only a few months, they thought they had found a three-chain helix. But, to their disappointment, the duo slowly realized that their model was flawed. It did not stand up to scientific examination. Further work on DNA was delayed as they returned to their respective research duties at Cambridge.

Chemical bonds. On Christmas of 1951 Crick gave Watson a copy of Linus Pauling's book *The Nature of the Chemical Bond*. (For his work on this subject, Pauling would later win the Nobel Prize in chemistry.) Chemical bonds are the electrical forces that link atoms together to form molecules. Certain bonds are formed when atoms share electrons, which orbit atomic nuclei. Normally, each atom has a certain number of electrons of its own. When it bonds in this way to another atom, however, one or more of these electrons are "shared" by both atoms, thereby holding the atoms together. The laws governing such bonds are very complicated, and Watson clearly needed to get a better grip on them before going further with his study of DNA.

At the same time, Watson began work on another subject, the tobacco mosaic virus (TMV). This virus contains RNA, or ribonucleic acid, a close relative of DNA. (Both are called nucleic acids because they are found in the cell's nucleus.) Watson began to suspect that RNA helps DNA do its job of protein-building. He used his research on the virus as a "front" to "mask" his continued interest in DNA (Watson, p. 67). In June 1952 Watson's X-ray crystallography work showed that TMV had a helix structure.

Pauling's mistake. Peter Pauling, Linus Pauling's son, was also studying in Cambridge and had become friends with Watson

▲ Watson conducted biology class as usual the day it was announced he won the 1962 Nobel Prize for medicine; one of his students, who arrived before the professor, shared the news with the class.

and Crick. That fall, he received a letter from his father that threw the two researchers into a depression. "In addition to routine family gossip," Watson wrote, "was the long-feared news that Linus now had a structure for DNA" (Watson, p. 91). Panic-stricken, they waited to hear the official word.

Finally, the paper arrived in which Pauling gave the details. His structure was a three-chain helix similar to that which Watson and Crick had arrived at the previous year. As he read the paper, however, Watson "felt something was not right" (Watson, p. 93). He and Crick soon figured out that Pauling, one of the world's leading authorities on chemistry, had overlooked a basic problem with the chemical bonds in his model. They realized that if they kept quiet, his mistake would take a while to be discovered. That would buy them time to complete their own study of the molecule.

The double helix. Watson concentrated on the models—trying out various ways of putting the atoms together—while Crick checked to see if the molecular model fit together in a way that made sense according to the laws of chemistry and math. Convinced that DNA's basic structure was that of a helix, they tried helical coils with one, two, three, and even four chains woven together. By late 1952 Watson was focusing on two-chain models, for the simple reason that things often come in pairs in biology.

Rosalind Franklin

Perhaps a major breakthrough in the discovery of the structure of DNA stemmed from Watson and Crick's collaboration with Rosalind Franklin. Franklin was an X-ray specialist who had taken much clearer pictures of DNA crystals than either of the two men. Watson and Crick used the information gathered by Franklin to complete their research.

After months of disappointment, Watson finally came up with a double helix model of DNA. This form allowed the building blocks of DNA—sugars, phosphates, and pairs of substances known as bases—to form bonds in a regular sequence. Crick checked the atomic connections one by one to see if they were correct. This time, the chemistry worked out.

Aftermath

Nobel Prize. Watson and Crick—their names now linked forever—won the Nobel Prize for medicine in 1962 for their work on DNA. (They shared the prize with Maurice Wilkins.) Watson continued his successful career in research and teaching, serving as a professor of biology at Harvard University from 1955 to 1976. In 1968, at the age of forty, he married Elizabeth Lewis, with whom he later had two sons, Rufus Robert and Duncan James. That same year, he became director of the Cold Spring Harbor Laboratory on Long Island, New York, and published his account of the discovery that made him famous, *The Double Helix*. A witty and often sarcastic look at the human side of the scientists' world, *The Double Helix* stirred up considerable controversy in scientific circles.

Watson also attracted attention in the early 1990s, when he resigned as director of the Human Genome Project, a highly publicized attempt to map the human genome, or the complete set of human genes. The project, heavily funded by the U.S. Congress, is an attempt to break the code by which the DNA chains hold their information. With typical honesty, Watson told a *Time* magazine interviewer that he had "no respect" for his boss on the project. In 1993 Watson and Crick reunited for a fortieth anniversary celebration of their discovery.

For More Information

"Happy Birthday, Double Helix." *Time,* March 15, 1993, pp. 56-59.

Watson, James. *The Double Helix.* Originally published in 1968. New York: Norton, 1980.

Expanding the Humanities

1943
▼
Akira Kurosawa writes and directs his first film, *Sanshiro Sugata.*

1944
▼
Leonard Bernstein introduces three compositions in New York: *Symphony No. 1, Fancy Free,* and *On the Town.*

1957
▼
Bernstein's *West Side Story* hits Broadway.

1953
▼
James Baldwin publishes *Go Tell It on the Mountain.*

1951
▼
Kurosawa's *Rashomon* wins the grand prize at the Venice Film Festival and an Academy Award for best foreign film.

1958
▼
Bernstein becomes musical director of the New York Philharmonic Orchestra.

1960
▼
Kurosawa's film *The Seven Samurai* is remade in the United States as *The Magnificent Seven.*

1975
▼
Kurosawa's *Dersu Uzala* wins grand prize at the Moscow Film Festival.

1985
▼
James Baldwin publishes his last major work, *The Evidence of Things Not Seen,* before his death in France two years later.

1980
▼
Kurosawa's *Kagemusha* wins the Golden Palm Award at the Cannes Film Festival.

EXPANDING THE HUMANITIES

Even before the end of World War II, great minds were exploring new areas of thought, and bold leaders were taking art in new directions. New ideas, different perspectives, and diverse influences converged with innovative styles and methods in the arts and humanities of Europe, Asia, and the United States. Three men are exemplary as leaders in these fields: Japanese filmmaker **Akira Kurosawa;** American musician **Leonard Bernstein;** and American writer **James Baldwin,** who was living in exile in France.

Kurosawa. Akira Kurosawa was attracted to Western art and cinema at an early age. He became intrigued with the American western film genre and its European (mainly Italian) equivalent, the so-called "spaghetti western." By the age of twenty-six, Kurosawa had decided to become a filmmaker and a scriptwriter. He wrote and directed "samurai films"—dramas much like American westerns, except they featured Japanese swordsmen instead of gunslingers from the American West. He continues to make social statements through film and introduces elements of classical literature to Japanese filmgoers.

Kurosawa was not recognized outside of Japan until his samurai scripts gained notice in Hollywood. The script for his

▲ **Akira Kurosawa make social statements through film and introduces elements of classical literature to Japanese filmgoers.**

1954 movie *The Seven Samurai* served as the basis for the 1960 American film *The Magnificent Seven.* Since the 1950s, Kurosawa has earned top international honors for his contributions to film.

Bernstein. Around the same time, a young American named Leonard Bernstein was dedicating himself to a career in music. A graduate of the Curtis Institute of Music, Bernstein had already begun to compose when he took his first major job as assistant conductor of the New York Philharmonic. He had a gift for making classical music accessible to the average American listener, but he also had success writing Broadway musicals such as *West Side Story.*

Baldwin. As Bernstein was composing Broadway smashes, a young writer from Harlem began to write about his bisexuality and his experiences growing up black in white America. James Baldwin's writings are filled with anger and passion: unable to live with American prejudices, he felt compelled to move abroad and settled in France.

Baldwin's powerful works called attention to the racial and sexual discrimination pervading America in the second half of the twentieth century. His first novel, *Go Tell It on the Mountain,* is about growing up black in New York. It is widely considered his best work. In addition, Baldwin wrote several other novels, story collections, an array of essays, and plays about social issues. His last work, *The Evidence of Things Not Seen,* is an exploration of the American court system.

Akira Kurosawa

1910-

Personal Background

Childhood and early education. The youngest of seven children, Akira Kurosawa was born in Tokyo, Japan, in 1910. His father, a former officer in the Japanese army, was a strict disciplinarian who demanded that his sons practice rigorous physical education.

Kurosawa attended Edogawa Elementary School, where he was introduced to the world of fine arts by a teacher named Tachikawa. Tachikawa took a special interest in exposing his young students to art and invited them to his home for discussions. He was Kurosawa's first profound artistic influence and convinced him to further his art education. Many of Japan's aspiring artists traveled overseas to study, but Kurosawa's family was not able to finance such a trip. Instead Kurosawa enrolled in the Doshusha School to study Western (mainly American and western European) painting.

Early works and influences. After graduating from Doshusha, Kurosawa landed jobs painting pictures for women's magazines and illustrating romance novels. He was recognized early on for his talent and was twice selected to participate in Tokyo's prestigious Nika Exhibition. As his art evolved, Kurosawa joined the Japan Proletariat Artists Group, a Marxist-influenced association for artists and writers. (Marxism is a political,

▲ **Akira Kurosawa**

Event: Bringing worldwide recognition to Japanese film.

Role: Akira Kurosawa of Japan is one of the most acclaimed filmmakers of the twentieth century. His motion pictures synthesize Japanese and American cultural influences in an attempt to resolve the eternal human conflict between good and evil.

economic, and social theory based on the philosophy of German intellectual Karl Marx, who advocated a classless society.) This group opposed the government and art institutions of Japan and championed new movements in art.

Kurosawa's older brother Heigo was another major influence on the fledgling artist. He, too, was artistic and a lover of film. Heigo was a film narrator who specialized in Japanese narrations for silent foreign films. A sensitive man known for his psychological depth, Heigo also had a lighter side: he introduced Kurosawa to Japanese vaudeville, known as "yose" and "kodan," a form of storytelling involving traditional samurai tales. (Heigo later killed himself, leaving Akira devastated. The bloody conflict in many of Akira Kurosawa's movies is, say some critics, a reaction to his brother's tragic death.)

Ravaging Earthquake

The tragic earthquake that rocked Tokyo in 1923 had a major impact on Kurosawa and his perception of the world. The death, blood, and despair that he witnessed fueled many of the violent scenes in his films.

At the age of twenty-six, Kurosawa earned his first break in the film industry. He was hired as a screenwriter and assistant director at P.C.L., a major Japanese film studio. After months of frustration and little, if any, real involvement in filmmaking, Kurosawa finally had an opportunity to work with Kajiro Yamamoto, a veteran Japanese director. Yamamoto was Kurosawa's first and only film teacher, and he insisted that the apprentice director learn to write scripts as well. Kurosawa's writings were full of images and noted for their attempts to separate what was real from what was false.

Kurosawa was still working as an assistant director when he published his first screenplay, *The Daruma Temple,* in 1941. His next screenplay, *All Is Quiet,* won the Nihon Eiga contest for best scenario and was also awarded a prize by the Minister of Education. It was not filmed, however, because it did not fulfill the government's wartime needs. Kurosawa worked on several Yamamoto films and became increasingly anxious to direct his own film. After a seven-year apprenticeship, he was promoted to full director at the studio and offered the opportunity to make his first feature.

Participation: Bringing Worldwide Recognition to Japanese Film

Kurosawa's first films. Kurosawa adapted the screenplay for his first feature-length film, 1943's *Sanshiro Sugata,* from a novel by Tsuneo Tomita. Although he directed the film himself, he did not have full production control. When *Sanshiro Sugata* was released in theaters, he was disappointed to find that footage had been edited from the film without his knowledge. The extracted footage was never found. The American occupation of Japan following World War II added to his discouragement; several parts of the film were banned for being "too feudalistic" (meaning the film's portrayal of political, social, and economic relationships between different classes of society were considered backward or unprogressive). Government censorship of the arts was an issue that frustrated Kurosawa throughout his career.

Kurosawa directed several other films before *Drunken Angel* (his seventh) established him as an important Japanese director in 1948. The story, which touches on many themes and employs a wide range of film techniques, deals with the miseries and fears of life in postwar Tokyo. Kurosawa is said to have considered it the first film in which he was truly able to express himself. He claimed total responsibility for the final film—it was his and no one else's. The next year, *Stray Dog* was released to wide acclaim. It was largely influenced by the style of Belgian crime novelist Georges Simenon and received an award from the Ministry of Education.

> ## Uniting the Japanese Film Industry
>
> As his first films were being produced and released, Kurosawa joined his mentor Yamamoto and others to form the Motion Picture Artists Association. This organization, which provided Japanese film writers, producers, directors, and actors with a united forum, came into being in response to a strike at P.C.L. (later known as Toho Films).

The samurai style. Much of Kurosawa's work draws on Japan's samurai (warrior) tradition. He contributed significantly to the development of the Japanese cinematic form known as the "samurai film." These motion pictures were based on the old Japanese ruling class system but resembled American westerns or Italian "spaghetti westerns," inexpensive European motion pictures with western themes and settings. There was always a

▲ **A scene from *The Seven Samurai*,** Kurosawa's film about samurai warriors who protect a sixteenth-century Japanese farming town from murderous bandits.

struggle between good and evil in these westerns, with the competing characters clearly identified. But Kurosawa's samurai films did not mark the boundaries between good and evil as distinctly as American westerns.

Several of Kurosawa's works inspired remakes. *The Seven Samurai,* a 1954 film about samurai warriors who protect a sixteenth-century Japanese farming town from murderous bandits, was the basis for the 1960 American western classic *The Magnificent Seven,* starring Steve McQueen, Yul Brynner, and Charles Bronson. Kurosawa's box office hit *Yojimbo* was remade by Italian director Sergio Leone (the king of the spaghetti westerns) as *A Fistful of Dollars,* starring Clint Eastwood as a gunslinger for hire. *Fistful,* released in 1964, defined the spaghetti western genre and made Eastwood a star.

Hollywood. In 1966 Kurosawa signed a film contract with

Hollywood producer Joseph Levin and left Japan, seeking greater artistic freedom in the West. Although this agreement resulted in his first color film project, Kurosawa's experience in Hollywood was disheartening. *The Runaway Train,* which was to be his first color film, was never completed because of its enormous budgeting problems. He began work on another film entitled *Tora! Tora! Tora!,* chronicling the Japanese bombing of Pearl Harbor, but again—because of the spiraling costs and disagreements that erupted on the set—Kurosawa was taken off the project and another director was hired to complete the film.

Soviet support. Disillusioned by filmmaking in the United States, Kurosawa returned to Japan in 1968. Japanese critics who resented his Westernized style were especially hard on him in the late 1960s. Kurosawa cracked under the psychological pressure and attempted suicide in 1971. After recovering from his injuries, he accepted the invitation of the Russian government to work on *Dersu Uzala,* a film based on the life of a Russian scholar who specialized in race relations. Shot in Siberia over a two-year schedule, *Dersu Uzala* won critical recognition in Japan, Russia, and the West. It received the Academy Award for best foreign-language film of 1975, as well as the gold medal at the Ninth Moscow International Film Festival.

Social themes. The complex and not always clearly defined nature of good and evil is one of the major themes explored in Kurosawa's films. Kurosawa is often characterized as a Western-influenced director whose works portray people trying to change the world. He depicts people in the midst of moral and philosophical development, engaging in struggles to come to terms with the conflicts in their lives. In his films, the hero—though constantly combatting evil—is not seen as perfect. Kurosawa's movies stress

---

Critical Acclaim

Several productions filmed in the 1950s are considered among Kurosawa's most important movies. *Rashomon,* a story about the complex nature of truth and honesty, was based on two short stories by Japanese writer Ryunosuke Akutagawa. The film received lukewarm reviews during its first run in Japan. However, it was met in the West with unanimous widespread acclaim, winning the Grand Prize at the Venice Film Festival and the Academy Award for best foreign film in 1951.

The 1952 motion picture *Ikiru,* one of Kurosawa's personal favorites, was immediately recognized in Japan and abroad as a major work. The film deals with the issue of identity and the problem of living in contemporary Japan. It won the David O. Selznick "Golden Laurel."

▲ A scene from *Ran,* Kurosawa's epic adaptation of Shakespeare's *King Lear;* the film centers on an aging warlord's decision to divide his kingdom among his three sons.

people's responsibilities to each other and to society; without illusion, they depict the gritty realism that all humans have to face.

Aftermath

In 1976 Kurosawa was named a "Person of Cultural Merits" by the Japanese government, making him the first person from the film profession to be awarded this honor. He continued to make films in the 1980s and 1990s. *Kagemusha* (title means "Shadow Warrior"), was made with the backing of American directors George Lucas and Francis Ford Coppola and won the Golden Palm Award at the 1980 Cannes Film Festival. Though diverse in subject matter, Kurosawa's later films share a certain intensity. *Ran,* released in 1985, is an epic adaptation of Shakespeare's *King Lear;* it centers on an aging warlord's decision to divide his kingdom among his three sons. The 1990 motion picture *Dreams* is an eerily spiritual film, and 1991's *Rhapsody in August* deals with the effects of the American bombing of Nagasaki, which brought World War II to its bloody close.

Kurosawa will be remembered for infusing his films with a sense of justice, dignity, and visual beauty. His memoir *Something Like an Autobiography* was published in 1984.

For More Information

Goodwin, James, editor. *Perspectives on Akira Kurosawa*. New York: McMillan International, 1994.

Kurosawa, Akira. *Something Like an Autobiography*. New York: Knopf, 1984.

Richie, Donald. *The Films of Akira Kurosawa*. Berkeley: University of California Press, 1984.

Filming the Classics

Some of Kurosawa's works brought literary classics to Japanese audiences. In 1951 he made a film based on Russian writer Fyodor Dostoyevsky's novel *The Idiot;* six years later, he released *The Throne of Blood,* based on William Shakespeare's *Macbeth.* But whether a foreign translation or his own creation, Kurosawa's movies almost always contain a hero and a villain. His characters are linked by their humanness, thus highlighting the importance of individual choice.

Leonard Bernstein

1918-1990

Personal Background

Early life. American conductor, pianist, and composer Leonard Bernstein was born August 25, 1918, in Lawrence, Massachusetts, a small town outside of Boston. He was the oldest of three children of Samuel and Jennie Resnick Bernstein, Russian immigrants who had journeyed to the United States to escape anti-Semitism (anti-Jewish sentiment) and seek economic opportunity and prosperity. Samuel had worked as a laborer in the Boston area for several years before opening the Samuel Bernstein Hair Company. The business grew, substantially improving the financial situation of the family, and Samuel dreamed of the day when Leonard would join the company and carry on the family name.

Discovering the world of music. But business held little interest for young Leonard, by all accounts a lonely and creative boy. Still, there was no early indication that music would be his great love. He took no unusual interest in music and had no music lessons as a young child. When he was ten years old, however, an aunt who had been living with the Bernsteins moved out, leaving her piano behind. Bernstein struck a few notes on the instrument and thought it sounded nice. It was not long before he was begging his mother to arrange for piano lessons. Soon he was studying with an instructor from the New England Conservatory of Music. The Conservatory then arranged for him to audition for

▲ Leonard Bernstein

Event: Advancing American music's international acceptance.

Role: Leonard Bernstein was one of the most prolific composers and outstanding conductors of the twentieth century. He is credited with promoting the works of American composers and popularizing classical music in the United States.

▲ By his mid-teens Bernstein had begun to show amazing creativity, composing his own works and organizing musical performances for family and friends.

Henrich Gebhard, the best piano teacher in Boston. Bernstein so impressed the renowned German musician that he accepted him as a pupil—despite the fact that Bernstein was unable to pay for the full tuition costs.

Teenage composer and producer. By his mid-teens Bernstein had begun to show amazing creativity, composing his own works and organizing musical performances for family and friends. He composed the school hymn for the prestigious Boston Latin High School, his alma mater, and organized successful productions of classical favorites at the Bernstein's summer home with the help of his younger sister, Shirley.

Musical preparations. Bernstein was an academic and a musical success. He seemed to excel at almost anything he tried—even becoming a star athlete in track and field. Bernstein graduated from Boston Latin at age sixteen and entered Harvard University the following year. There was no question that music would be his main concentration, and he immediately began studying under Walter Piston, a prominent American composer and teacher. The university provided opportunities for Bernstein to write and perform his music and to meet the leading members of the music world, including Dimitri Mitropoulos, the guest conductor of the Boston Symphony Orchestra, and Aaron Copland, the famed American composer.

As he neared graduation from Harvard in April 1939, Bernstein made his debut by conducting a composition he had written for *Aristophanes,* a Greek play. A month later, he conducted the piece "The Cradle Will Rock." He then moved to New York, a haven for musicians, artists, and actors, and continued to work on his music, writing songs and performing in nightclubs. Later in 1939, with the help of Mitropoulos, he began a two-year program at the well-known Curtis Institute, where he made his symphonic conducting appearance with *Second Symphony,* a piece written by his tutor and the institute director, Randall Thompson.

Invitation to Tanglewood. In 1940 Bernstein was invited to participate in the young musicians' program at Tanglewood, the summer home of the Boston Symphony Orchestra. The orchestra's conductor, Sergei Koussevitzky, had recently opened the Berkshire Music Center, a summer school where young musicians could study with great conductors and teachers, conduct student orchestras and choirs, and hear their own compositions performed. Bernstein spent two summers at Tanglewood and was later hired as a teaching assistant. It was during this time that he began to write the vocal section for *Lamentations for Jeremiah,* a piece based on a Hebrew text.

An American success story. In 1943, at the age of twenty-five, Bernstein was appointed assistant conductor of the New York Philharmonic Orchestra. He had only conducted the orchestra twice when, on November 14, 1943, a chance event brought him fame.

Bernstein was attending a performance by a Russian singer on a Saturday afternoon when he received word that Bruno Walter, who was supposed to be guest conducting the New York Philharmonic Orchestra the next evening, had become ill. Even though he had practically no experience, the young assistant conductor knew he would have to lead the orchestra himself. He was nervous, particularly because there was no time to call the orchestra together for a rehearsal. He reportedly rushed home and stayed up until early in the morning going over every note in the presentation planned for a packed Carnegie Hall.

Bernstein's Success at Carnegie Hall

Before Bernstein's Carnegie Hall performance, the most prestigious orchestras had been conducted only by foreigners, and most American musicians had been trained at renowned European conservatories. Among music critics and symphony audiences a feeling prevailed that American training—even American culture itself—could not produce world-class symphony conductors. Bernstein's acclaimed performance forced many music lovers to rethink this prejudicial view.

When young Bernstein took the floor that evening, the concert audience's initial reaction was one of skepticism. However, the flawless, passionate performance so roused the conservative Philharmonic audience that he received a standing ovation. Music critics were wowed. Bernstein instantly became a star in the international music world. It was an enormous triumph in the field of classical music for an American-born, native-trained musician.

Participation: Advancing American Music's International Acceptance

Composer. The following year, Bernstein exploded into the ranks of world-class composers by unveiling three major (and markedly different) musical works: a symphony titled *Jeremiah,* the ballet *Fancy Free,* and a Broadway musical, *On the Town.* (*On the Town* was adapted for the stage from the jazzy *Fancy Free.*)

These three hits from 1944 illustrated Bernstein's great range of talent.

From his dramatic 1944 successes, Bernstein went on to compose masterpieces of both classical and popular music. He would eventually announce—but never really carry out—his intention to stop conducting altogether and concentrate strictly on composing.

Promoting American music worldwide. In 1945 Bernstein was asked to direct the newly founded New York Symphony Orchestra. This position gave him the authority to plan the symphony's musical programs. Under his direction, the orchestra presented a program specializing in contemporary music with an American emphasis. Bernstein was also invited by his friend and mentor, Sergei Koussevitzky, to guest-conduct the Boston Symphony Orchestra several times in Boston and at Tanglewood.

In a typical Bernstein presentation, both European and American compositions were featured prominently. Other symphony orchestras began to pattern their performances after those of Bernstein. Previously, these musical groups had chosen only from the works of a select group of seventeenth- and eighteenth-century European composers such as Ludwig van Beethoven, Wolfgang Amadeus Mozart, and Joseph Haydn. Including American compositions in the repertoires of prestigious orchestras further exposed the elite classical music world to the talents of American composers.

> ### Some of Bernstein's Compositions
>
> Among Bernstein's works are the symphonies *Jeremiah,* 1944, *Kaddish,* 1946, and *The Age of Anxiety,* 1949; the musicals *On the Town,* 1944, *Wonderful Town,* 1952, *Candide,* 1956, and *West Side Story,* 1957; and the operas *Trouble in Tahiti,* 1952, and *A Quiet Place,* 1983.

Conducting American music abroad. In the spring of 1946 Bernstein took American music to the halls of Europe. He represented the United States at the Prague International Music Festival, playing American and American-influenced works, including his own *Jeremiah* symphony, Aaron Copland's *El Salon Mexico,* and Robert Schumann's *American Festival Overture.* He also conducted the London Philharmonic in the debut of his own *Appalachian Spring.*

▲ Bernstein wanted to make the music that he loved accessible to the public, particularly young people.

In the late 1940s Bernstein spent a great deal of time guest conducting with the Israeli Philharmonic Orchestra. From 1958 to 1969 he served as the musical director of the New York Philharmonic.

The Youngest Conductor

Bernstein was the first American (and the youngest person ever) to conduct at the Teatro della Scala in Milan, making his debut at the renowned theater with the famed opera singer Maria Callas.

Bringing music to the masses. Bernstein wanted to make the music that he loved accessible to the public, particularly young people. To further this goal, he initiated a series of symphonic lectures for the Canadian Broadcasting Company in 1954. This was followed by public appearances in Europe, the Soviet Union, and South America. Bernstein became famous for his performances and lectures on American music. He even appeared on television, introducing the *Young People's Concerts* to American audiences.

Aftermath

Bernstein is remembered as one of America's most versatile, prominent, and respected musicians. In addition, he used his fame, his music, and his writings to raise consciousness about pressing global issues. In 1983 he urged musicians, music lovers, and friends to mark his sixty-fifth birthday by organizing a demonstration in support of a worldwide nuclear freeze. The demonstration was observed in the United States, Europe, South America, Japan, and Israel.

With the help of a National Fellowship Award, Bernstein embarked on peace tours with the Western European Youth Orchestra to commemorate the fortieth anniversary of the bombing of Hiroshima, the devastating and controversial attack on Japan by the United States that ended World War II. In 1989 he conducted three performances of Beethoven's Ninth Symphony in recognition of the fall of the Berlin Wall (a concrete wall that had divided the German city of Berlin into two sections—East Berlin in the former communist republic of East Germany, and West Berlin in the former capitalist republic of West Germany—for nearly three decades). Bernstein died in 1990 while working on a new composition, *Babel*.

Bernstein on Broadway

Bernstein continued his Broadway successes in the 1950s with musicals such as *Wonderful Town*, a hit that played for 500 performances in New York. His biggest Broadway triumph, however, came in 1957 with *West Side Story*, a musical play adapted from the Arthur Laurents tale of love tainted by gang rivalry. It was a work that drew together the greatest talents in American music—choreographed by Jerome Robbins, with lyrics written by Stephen Sondheim and music composed by Bernstein. *West Side Story*, widely regarded as an update of William Shakespeare's tragedy *Romeo and Juliet*, was adapted for film in 1961. It received ten Academy Awards.

For More Information

Bernstein, Leonard. *Findings*. New York: Simon & Schuster, 1982.

Gradenwitz, Peter. *Leonard Bernstein: The Infinite Variety of a Musician*. New York: Oswald Wolff, 1987.

Peyser, Joan. *Bernstein: A Biography*. New York: Beech Tree Books, 1987.

James Baldwin

1924-1987

Personal Background

Early childhood. James Baldwin was born in New York City's Harlem on August 2, 1924. He was the eldest of nine children, and throughout his early life he would be largely responsible for the care of his siblings. Baldwin's stepfather, an evangelical preacher with a hard heart and even harder fists, had moved north to escape racial oppression in New Orleans, Louisiana. The family lived in severe poverty, often relying on government assistance just to survive.

Baldwin became involved in the church at an early age, partly to escape from the menacing world of drugs and crime that surrounded him. At the age of fourteen, he became a youth minister at the Fireside Pentecostal Assembly. Small in stature but with fiery eyes and a powerful and convincing voice, he was soon one of the most capable ministers on the church staff.

As a teenage preacher, Baldwin suffered from immense inner conflicts—conflicts between his father, who had an intense hatred for whites, and his own growing friendships as a student with white classmates in an intellectually stimulating school environment, and conflicts between his traditional Christian ideals and his own bisexuality. The anger that tainted most of Baldwin's life and his writings eventually persuaded him to leave his successful life as a Christian minister:

▲ **James Baldwin**

Event: Expanding and popularizing black literature.

Role: A prolific writer and chronicler of the struggle for civil rights, James Baldwin expanded the world of black and American literature with works that explore the impact of race and sexuality in American society.

A truly moral human being ... must first divorce himself from all the prohibitions, crimes, and hypocrisies of the Christian church. If the concept of God has any validity, or any use, it can only be to make us larger, freer, and more loving. If God cannot do this, then it is time we got rid of Him. (Baldwin 1962, p. 61)

Difficult Childhood

Baldwin's stepfather enforced strict "Christian" ideals in a twisted way—by beating his children. Baldwin was a successful writer and a mature adult before understanding that his stepfather was motivated by shame and despair: the elder Baldwin could not provide adequately for his children—and sometimes could not even muster up enough money to feed them.

Early literary beginnings. As a child, Baldwin was an avid reader with an immense love of books. As early as junior high school, his teachers recognized his talents and put him to work on the school literary magazine. He continued to write throughout his high school years, serving as the editor of the school newspaper in his senior year. A friendship he struck up with Beanford Delaney, an African American painter, had an enormous influence on him. Delaney was a symbol of African American success in the arts. He became a mentor to the young Baldwin, introducing him to jazz and teaching him the artist's skill of seeing.

Participation: Expanding and Popularizing Black Literature

New Jersey and Greenwich Village. With the costs of college way out of his reach, Baldwin worked in New Jersey for a year after graduating from high school. It was there that he encountered southern-style racism in restaurants and bars, at work, and on the streets. He would remember the effects of these "Jim Crow" experiences (legalized racial segregation and discrimination) later in one of his most popular works, *Notes of a Native Son.* Meanwhile, he began writing the novel *Crying Holy,* a book that attempted to reconcile the role of the church and his father in his own life.

In 1944 Baldwin moved to Greenwich Village, a section of Manhattan that was a haven for artists, writers and musicians. There he found a job as a waiter in a West Indian restaurant, working hours that allowed him time for writing. It was in the Village

▲ James Baldwin expanded the world of black and American literature with works that explore the impact of race and sexuality in American society.

that Baldwin first met Richard Wright, author of the critically acclaimed novel *Native Son* and, at the time, the most successful black writer in the world. Wright supported Baldwin, aiding him with funding to complete his *Crying Holy* manuscript and then passing it along to his publisher, Harper and Brothers. He also helped the struggling young writer obtain a $500 Eugene F. Saxton fellowship. The support for *Crying Holy* was the first financial compensation Baldwin had ever received for his writing. However, the manuscript was ultimately rejected.

Literary Influences on Baldwin's Writings

Two authors greatly influenced Baldwin's development during the late 1940s. As a young man, Baldwin had read Harriet Beecher Stowe's *Uncle Tom's Cabin* and Richard Wright's *Native Son* over and over, absorbing these accounts of the evils of slavery and the difficulties young black men faced growing up in America. At first these authors were models for Baldwin, but as he developed his own style in Paris, he began to view the Stowe and Wright characters as two-dimensional and thus too limited. Baldwin wrote critiques of the two books. The publication of his ideas led to a falling out between Baldwin and Wright, who felt that Baldwin had publicly rejected his novel.

Despite his criticism of *Native Son*, Baldwin was profoundly moved by Wright's literary work. Though built on simple plots, Wright's novels were marked by deep explorations of his characters' consciousness, their doubts, and their motivations. Baldwin's writings and characters clearly reflect this emphasis.

Wright also introduced Baldwin to other writers and editors at Village bars and restaurants. These contacts ultimately led to magazine assignments at prominent journals such as *The Nation, Commentary, Partisan Review,* and *New Leader.* In 1947 Baldwin's first article, a review of a collection of Russian short stories, was published in *The Nation.* A year later, he published "Harlem Ghetto: Winter 1948," his first full essay, and "Previous Condition," his first short story, in *Commentary.*

Escape to Paris. Later in 1948 Baldwin was awarded a Rosenwald fellowship. The money from the award allowed him to leave the United States for Paris, France. Although it had its own race and class distinctions, Paris provided an escape from the racial oppression of the United States. Baldwin saw the French city as a place where he could truly find his voice as a writer and come to terms with his own racial and sexual identity.

Early works. In 1952 Baldwin finished *Crying Holy,* which had been renamed *Go Tell It on the Mountain,* for the mountain upon which he wrote it in the Swiss village of Loeche-les-Bains. He sent the manuscript to New York, where it was accepted by the Alfred Knopf publishing company. The following year, it was published by Knopf and received widespread critical acclaim.

With the help of a Guggenheim fellowship, Baldwin went on to write his first play, titled *The Amen Corner,* and began two novels, *Giovanni's Room* and *Another Country.* In 1955 he published *Notes of a Native Son,* a collection of essays on the experience of being a black male in the racially oppressive United States. That same year he finished *Giovanni's Room,* a book that was innovative in both its content—a homosexual love affair—and its characters—who were white.

Baldwin wrote with an angry passion that crossed racial lines, touching readers of all colors. Some of the deep emotions in the author's works stem from his own search for his sexual identity. In addition to *Giovanni's Room,* Baldwin penned other stories that explored the complexity of human sexuality, including 1962's *Another Country,* which deals with the painful nature of love—straight and gay, black and white. It was tremendously well received by critics and audiences alike and was awarded recognition from the National Council of Christians and Jews. Another novel, *Tell Me How Long the Train's Been Gone,* examines the cost of fame for a successful black bisexual actor.

From 1956 until 1985 Baldwin continued to write about his own experiences and observations of the evils of prejudice, both racial and sexual. He became known as one of the most powerful contemporary writers of fiction and nonfiction. Baldwin viewed Christianity, whiteness, imperialism (the extension of a nation's power beyond its own borders), and democratic institutions with suspicion and warned whites about the destructive effects of rampant racial intolerance in America. His essays from the 1950s and 1960s show that he pitied racist whites as well as the victims of their hatred:

> Furthermore, the white man knows his history, knows himself to be a devil, and knows that his time is running out, and all his technology, psychology, science, and "tricknology" are being expended in the effort to prevent black men from hearing the truth. (Baldwin 1962, p. 80)

In 1961 and 1963, Baldwin published two books about the civil rights movement that established him as the era's most important

African American writer: *Nobody Knows My Name* and *The Fire Next Time. Nobody Knows My Name* deals with what it means to be black in America and questions the country's true national identity; *The Fire Next Time,* a collection of previously published magazine articles, is an attempt to make whites feel some of the anger and pain of blacks in America.

Some Other Works by Baldwin

Go Tell It on the Mountain (novel), 1953.

Notes of a Native Son (magazine essays), 1955.

Another Country (novel), 1962.

Blues for Mister Charlie (play), produced and published in 1964.

Going to Meet the Man (short stories), 1965.

The Amen Corner (play; first produced in 1955), published in 1968.

Tell Me How Long the Train's Been Gone (novel), 1968.

If Beale Street Could Talk (novel), 1974.

The Devil Finds Work (essays), 1976.

Little Man, Little Man (children's fiction), 1976.

The Evidence of Things Not Seen (nonfiction), 1985.

Aftermath

Declining literary influence. By 1962, when *Another Country* was published, Baldwin had reached the peak of his literary prominence. He continued to write but devoted most of his energies in subsequent years to involvement with the civil rights movement.

***Harper's* and civil rights.** In September 1957, having returned to the United States, Baldwin was commissioned by *Harper's* magazine to write an article about the fight for civil rights in the South. In researching his article, which he titled "A Hard Kind of Courage," he traveled to Charlotte, North Carolina, where protesters had begun their program of civil disobedience (a nonviolent refusal to obey government rules). He then journeyed across the South from Birmingham and Tuskegee, Alabama, to Little Rock, Arkansas.

Baldwin considered his writing to be a worthy contribution to the movement and strove to raise the racial consciousness of all people. He also became a leading fund-raiser and speaker for equality. Still, many leaders of the civil rights movement embraced the idea of black separatism (a division between black and white segments of society) rather than multiculturalism and therefore rejected Baldwin and his ideas. Some observers attribute these hard feelings to Baldwin's insistence on calling himself an "American writer" rather than a "black writer"—and to his continued appeals for change within the white community.

Later writings. Although Baldwin wrote until his death in 1987, some of the fire of his writing vanished in his later years. The flames of the early anger that ran through his books began to die down in the late 1960s. From the publication of *If Beale Street Could Talk* in 1974 to his death in 1987, Baldwin only published about a half dozen books, including *Just above My Head* and *Evidence of Things Not Seen* (the latter being an expanded version of a *Playboy* article about child murders in Atlanta and the young black man accused of the crimes). He also wrote a screenplay on the life of civil rights martyr Malcolm X titled *One Day, When I Was Lost,* which served as the basis for Spike Lee's acclaimed feature film *X.* In his later years, Baldwin spent time as a university lecturer on racial issues. He died in France on November 30, 1987.

For More Information

Baldwin, James. *The Fire Next Time.* New York: Dial, 1962.

Baldwin, James. *Just above My Head.* New York: Dial, 1979.

Kenan, Randall. *James Baldwin.* New York: Chelsea House, 1994.

O'Daniel, Therman B. *James Baldwin: A Critical Evaluation.* Washington, DC: Howard University Press, 1977.

Sylvander, Carolyn. *James Baldwin.* New York: Frederick Ungar, 1980.

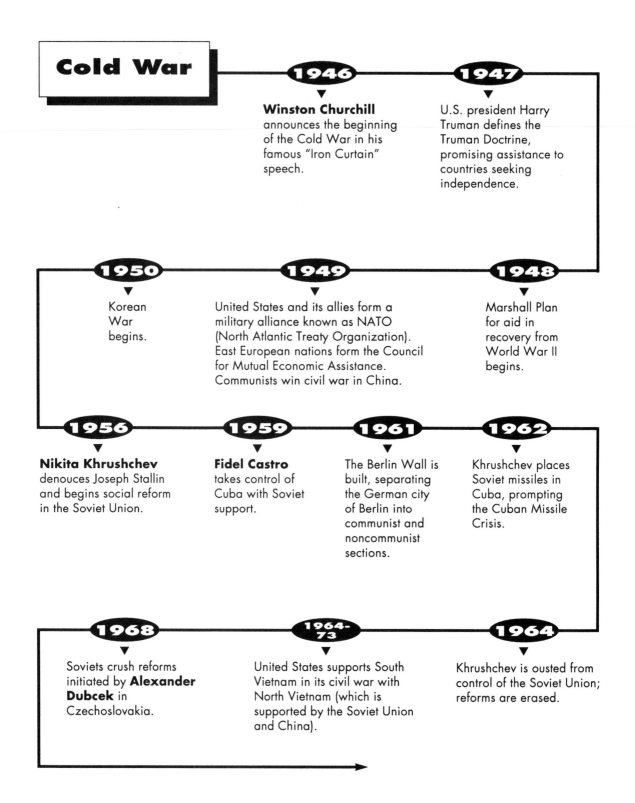

Cold War

1946
Winston Churchill announces the beginning of the Cold War in his famous "Iron Curtain" speech.

1947
U.S. president Harry Truman defines the Truman Doctrine, promising assistance to countries seeking independence.

1950
Korean War begins.

1949
United States and its allies form a military alliance known as NATO (North Atlantic Treaty Organization). East European nations form the Council for Mutual Economic Assistance. Communists win civil war in China.

1948
Marshall Plan for aid in recovery from World War II begins.

1956
Nikita Khrushchev denouces Joseph Stallin and begins social reform in the Soviet Union.

1959
Fidel Castro takes control of Cuba with Soviet support.

1961
The Berlin Wall is built, separating the German city of Berlin into communist and noncommunist sections.

1962
Khrushchev places Soviet missiles in Cuba, prompting the Cuban Missile Crisis.

1968
Soviets crush reforms initiated by **Alexander Dubcek** in Czechoslovakia.

1964-73
United States supports South Vietnam in its civil war with North Vietnam (which is supported by the Soviet Union and China).

1964
Khrushchev is ousted from control of the Soviet Union; reforms are erased.

COLD WAR

After World War I the political map of Europe was redrawn. Old nations were realigned and new ones were created in the hopes of balancing powers and spheres of influence. Two decades later, during World War II, Britain, France, the United States, and the Soviet Union came together for a common purpose—to block the forces of Germany and its associates. But after the war, serious questions of global control needed to be addressed.

The "iron curtain." Less than a year after the war ended, Britain's prime minister, **Winston Churchill,** revealed the new world order, defining the postwar terms of worldwide political and economic influence. He gave a now-famous speech at Fulton, Missouri, on March 5, 1946, declaring: "From Stettin in the Baltic to Trieste in the Adriatic, an iron curtain has descended across the continent" (Churchill in Spielvogel, p. 1022).

Soviet forces had played a significant role in breaking Nazi leader Adolf Hitler's horrific stranglehold on Europe, and in return the Soviet Union—then a great communist power—sought to extend its control throughout the continent. Soviet communism was an economic and political system rooted in a central government with unyielding strength. This dictatorial leadership controlled both the means of production and the distribution of goods throughout the Soviet Socialist Republics.

Beginning of the Cold War. The Soviets had taken over Poland, part of Germany, Czechoslovakia, Hungary, Romania, and Austria after World War II; they then threatened to dominate Greece and Yugoslavia. The Cold War had begun. (A cold war is a condition of extreme political tension between nations that falls short of a military conflict.)

In March 1947 U.S. president Harry Truman had announced his own plans for preserving democracy throughout the world. His Truman Doctrine and the plan for carrying it out—the Marshall Plan—would provide massive help for those nations devastated by the war and struggling to establish economic stability and a democratic government. The first Marshall Plan funds were given to Greece in an effort to draw a line against Soviet domination.

U.S.-Soviet tensions. Over the next quarter century, the United States and the Soviet Union practiced a diplomacy of "brinkmanship"—each testing the other over and over for world influence. Soviet chairman **Nikita Khrushchev** repeatedly challenged the will of European and American rulers. He attempted to unify a divided Germany and to install Soviet-style communism there. The wartime Allies had sectioned Germany so that parts of it were controlled by Britain, France, the United States, and the Soviet Union separately. A similar division of responsibility separated sections of the city of Berlin. Twice, in 1948 and again in 1958, the Soviets threatened the city in an attempt to wrest all of Germany from capitalist control. (Capitalism is an economic system based on private—rather than government—ownership and distribution of goods in a free and competitive market.)

The Soviet brand of communism, however, did not seem to suit all nations equally well. Installed by force in Czechoslovakia, communism was unpopular, and the Soviets soon found that the people of that country wanted a more liberal form of socialism. (Socialism is a political doctrine that champions the removal of private property in a quest to attain a classless society.) **Alexan-**

der Dubcek, the Soviet-appointed ruler of Czechoslovakia, came under fire and was quickly replaced by the Soviets when he attempted to liberalize Czech communism.

Worldwide conflict. The post-World War II maneuvers by these great powers spread into confrontations around the world. In the early 1950s the ongoing feud between communist North Korea and noncommunist South Korea erupted into war. That war brought U.S. troops into action against the North Koreans, who were closely allied with the communist Soviet Union and China. In the 1960s and 1970s a long struggle evolved over a similar division in Vietnam. Nearer the United States, confrontations between **Fidel Castro**'s Soviet-backed Cuba and the United States led to one of the most serious events of the Cold War—an attempt by the Soviet Union to place missiles on Cuban land.

In the mid-1960s the Cold War gave way to a frightening and expensive nuclear "arms race" between superpowers. The cost of this race seriously drained the resources of the United States, allowing nations such as China and Japan to increase their influence in world markets.

Winston Churchill

1874-1965

Personal Background

Destined for the military. Winston Leonard Spencer Churchill was born on November 30, 1874, in the ancestral palace of Blenheim in Oxfordshire (a county along the Thames River in south-central England). His father was Lord Randolph Churchill, the third son of the seventh duke of Marlborough. Lord Randolph was an active Conservative Party politician who became England's chancellor of the exchequer (secretary of the treasury). Churchill's mother was Jennie Jerome, an American and the daughter of a New York business tycoon.

From his childhood, Churchill seemed destined for a military career. Although he showed no real academic promise in the private school he attended at Harrow, he seemed fascinated by soldiers. He was also interested in history, particularly military history, and poetry. Once his studies at Harrow were completed, he immediately enrolled at Sandhurst, Britain's Royal Military Academy, from which he graduated in 1894. He became a junior officer in the Queen's Own Regiment, the Fourth Hussars. Churchill saw active duty in Cuba, India, Sudan, and Egypt. Much of the time, he coupled his military duty with writing or reporting for British newspapers.

Churchill was in South Africa as a reporter during the Boer struggle for independence from the British. (Boer is the name

▲ **Winston Churchill**

Event: Setting the conditions for the Cold War.

Role: During World War II, Winston Churchill saw the necessity of forming a partnership with the Soviet Union. Then, as the war ended in defeat for the forces of Germany, Italy, and Japan, he became one of the first to realize that the relationship between the Soviets and the Western allies would change dramatically.

given to South Africans of Dutch descent.) In 1899 he was captured by the Boers but escaped. Churchill's reporting of this escape brought him fame, and his army service had brought him some money—enough to enter English politics. Except for brief interludes devoted exclusively to writing, his political career would span the next sixty years.

Churchill proved his independence by switching political parties several times. He entered the British House of Commons in 1900 as a conservative, for example, but received his first ministerial appointment (in 1906) from a liberal government. Meanwhile, Churchill polished his wit and public speaking ability and developed a flair for the dramatic. When the leader of the Liberal Party, David Lloyd George, tried to reduce the power of the House of Lords, Churchill made one of his most sensational party changes, dramatically rising in the midst of a parliamentary session to cross over the aisle and take a seat by him.

Despite his conservative stances and his biting speeches, Churchill swiftly rose in the British government. And in the midst of this early career, Churchill took time in 1908 to marry Clementine Hozier. She provided a happy balance to his political turmoils for the rest of their lives together. By the time they were married, he had already published his first three books and was on his way to becoming a successful author.

The Many Sides of Churchill's Early Career

1900-04	Conservative member of the House of Commons representing Oldham.
1904-06	Liberal member of the House of Commons representing Oldham.
1905	Undersecretary for the colonies.
1906-08	Liberal Commoner representing Northwest Manchester.
1908-22	Conservative Commoner from Dundee.
1908	Made president of the Board of Trade by Liberal Prime Minister Herbert H. Asquith.
1910	Appointed home secretary.

Anticommunist beliefs. On whichever side of Parliament he sat, Churchill was an aggressive defender of British interests. In 1911 he was placed in charge of the admiralty and immediately began preparing the British navy for the already brewing war with Germany. When World War I came in 1914, the British navy was well prepared. Three years

▲ Churchill inspects the honor guard in London in June 1943. He had been a powerful and enthusiastic supporter of the development of a new weapon: the tank.

later, Churchill—by then minister of munitions—became a powerful and enthusiastic supporter of the development of a new weapon: the tank.

Churchill was a passionate anticommunist from the moment communism achieved its first victory in Russia. (Communism is a system of government in which the state controls the means of production and the distribution of goods.) After World War I, as secretary of war, his job was to supervise the demobilization of the large wartime armed forces. He proved to be a strong advocate of an Allied (the Western powers) intervention in Russia against the Bolsheviks. (The Bolsheviks were revolutionaries who organized the overthrow of the Russian government in 1917.)

Political outcast. In 1922 Churchill lost his seat in Parliament but was reelected two years later as a "constitutionalist." This time it was the conservative government led by Stanley Baldwin that offered him the high post of chancellor of the exchequer. His policies, however, soon made him unpopular, and he was dismissed by Baldwin. Disliked by all parties, Churchill spent the decade between 1929 and 1939 out of office.

Although he recognized very early on that Nazi leader Adolf Hitler's seizure of power in Germany was a grave threat to European security, Churchill was unable to rally support for his position. However, he had made his ideas heard, and when war broke out in 1940, British prime minister Neville Chamberlain reappointed him the first lord of the admiralty. Chamberlain was reluctant to take a stand against Germany's takeover of part of Czechoslovakia; he soon became so unpopular that he resigned. Churchill then became prime minister of Britain—putting him in a position to lead the government throughout World War II.

British bulldog. As a wartime leader, the cigar-smoking, growling Churchill immediately established himself as the living symbol of steely British determination. In order to defeat Hitler, he was willing to ally Britain not only with the United States but also with the communist Soviet Union. The bases for this "Grand Alliance" included an Anglo-American agreement (an agreement between Great Britain and the United States) made after the bombing of Pearl Harbor (the surprise Japanese attack on American forces in Hawaii on December 7, 1941, which brought the United States into World War II) and an Anglo-Soviet mutual assistance pact reached in May 1942. During the war, Churchill, U.S. president Franklin Delano Roosevelt, and

Accepting the Prime Ministry

Winston Churchill became one of history's most dramatic speakers. When he accepted the prime ministry, he told Parliament, "I have nothing to offer but blood, toil, tears, and sweat." During the darkest hours of the German air bombardments of Britain, he rallied the British people by announcing, "We shall fight on the beaches, we shall fight on the fields and in the streets, we shall fight in the hills, we shall never surrender."

▲ As a wartime leader, the cigar-smoking, growling Churchill immediately established himself as the living symbol of steely British determination.

Soviet leader Joseph Stalin worked together and shared the common purpose of defeating Hitler's Germany.

Participation:
Setting the Conditions for the Cold War

Caution in dealing with the Soviets. Even before World War II ended, however, Churchill was pushing for action that would control the Soviets' ambitions. He tried to convince Roosevelt to undertake an Allied push into Eastern Europe as a means of limiting Soviet expansion into the area, but the American president refused. Roosevelt and his advisers were more inclined to trust the Soviet leaders. Moreover, prior to the actual dropping of the first atom bomb on Hiroshima, Japan, on August 6, 1945, the U.S. commanders were anxious to prevent any disagreement with the Soviets that might delay their participation in the final attack on Japan.

Greek civil war. Unable to convince the Americans to take joint measures to limit communist gains in Europe, Churchill was willing to act alone where he had the power. In December 1944, after the withdrawal of German forces, Greek communists attempted to seize power by force of arms; in response, Churchill quickly ordered British forces in Athens to disarm the rebels.

Iron curtain. Churchill reluctantly agreed to the postwar division of Europe, but he began to express grave concern about the impending demobilization of the British forces and the withdrawal of American troops from Europe while the Soviets remained with hundreds of divisions stationed in the occupied territory. He used the phrase "iron curtain" (meaning a barrier that isolates all Soviet or Soviet-controlled areas from the rest of the world) to describe the new Soviet uncooperativeness in a May 12, 1945 telegram to President Truman. Churchill emphasized the need to arrive at an understanding with the Soviets while Britain and the United States still had large numbers of troops in Europe. In 1945, however, the British were weary of war and wanted a change of leaders. Churchill was replaced as prime minister by Clement Atlee, a labor leader.

In the United States. In October 1945 Churchill received a note from Truman proposing that he deliver a series of speeches at Westminster College in Fulton, Missouri. Churchill sailed for an extended visit to the United States the next January. On February 9, however, before Churchill could begin his lectures, Stalin made a dramatic speech himself. No peaceful international order was possible, Stalin claimed, and the Soviet Union must devote its resources to rearmament and postpone any investment in the production of consumer goods. The position of the Soviet leader confirmed what Churchill had warned of all along.

The United States felt that while the Soviets could be expected to advance their power wherever possible, they would avoid direct confrontation because the recent war had weakened them. The American government supported a vigorous and unified Western response to Stalin's ambitions.

Train ride. On March 4, 1946, after visiting the White House, Churchill and Truman boarded a special train for the trip to Missouri. On the twenty-four-hour trip, Churchill put the finishing touches on his speech, which he titled "The Sinews of Peace." He showed the speech to Truman, who expressed approval of it.

The Fulton Speech. The speech was delivered March 5, 1946. In it, Churchill reminded his audience that the United States was at the peak of its power and that this entailed certain responsibilities. The recent Allied victory had become overshadowed by the threat of the Soviet Union. An "iron curtain" had descended upon the continent of Europe, stretching from "Stettin in the Baltic to Trieste in the Adriatic."

Many great European cities—Warsaw, Berlin, Prague, Vienna, Budapest, Belgrade, Bucharest, and Sofia—were now behind this curtain of communist influence. Already the Soviet-dominated Polish government had been encouraged to claim a large portion of German territory and expel millions of Germans from it. Small Communist parties had seized power in Eastern and Central Europe and were transforming their countries into police states. At war's end, British and American forces had pulled back 150 miles along a 400-mile front to allow the Red (Soviet) Army to occupy some of Germany. Here the Soviets were encouraging the establishment of a communist regime. "This," Churchill observed, "is not the liberated Europe we fought to build up. Nor is it one which contains the essentials of permanent peace."

> ## The Power of Speech and Pen
>
> Winston Churchill had worked many years to polish his speaking ability and had become a master of short speeches constructed on the spur of the moment. He was, however, still best at delivering a well-prepared, preplanned speech. Writing had helped make him an excellent speechwriter. Some early books by Churchill include *The River War* (1899); *Lord Randolph Churchill* (1906); *The World Crisis* (six volumes about World War I; 1922-31); and *My Early Life: A Roving Commission* (1930).

A Western alliance. Churchill expressed his belief that the Soviets did not desire war but wanted the fruits of war and the indefinite expansion of their power and doctrines. What was needed was a settlement negotiated from a position of strength, and this demanded the unity of Western democracies. Only a united West could hope to stand up to the Soviets and avert another war. A close alliance between the United States and Britain, he said, would ensure the security of the world for a century to come.

Aftermath

Setting the stage for relations with the Soviets. In 1946 many Americans still held to the possibility of cooperation with the Soviet Union. The immediate reaction to Churchill's speech was one of hostility. Several American Democratic senators called the speech shocking. The *Chicago Sun Times,* which only a week earlier had been eager to publish Churchill's wartime "Secret Session" speeches, called the latest speech poisonous and a proposal for world domination—through arms—by the United States and the British Empire.

Despite this initial negative reaction, Churchill's assessment of Soviet intentions—and his ideas about the proper means of countering them—would become the blueprint for the West's dealings with the Soviet Union. In 1947 the U.S. president unveiled what would become known as the Truman Doctrine, which put an end to U.S. isolation and promised military and economic assistance to any country wishing to protect its independence. This was quickly followed by the Marshall Plan, a massive American aid program designed to bring about European economic recovery, and the 1949 establishment of the North Atlantic Treaty Organization (NATO). NATO committed the Western democracies to collective defense against Soviet aggression and to economic and political cooperation. (Since the breakup of the Soviet Union in 1991, NATO's political and military goals have changed.)

Last years. Churchill became England's prime minister again after the 1951 election and served until his semi-retirement from politics in 1955. As long as he was active in politics, he was a strong advocate of European unity. His six-volume history of World War II appeared between 1948 and 1953, and his four-volume *History of the English-Speaking Peoples* between 1956 and 1958. He was awarded the Nobel Prize for literature in 1953. On April 9, 1963, the U.S. Congress made him an honorary American citizen. Churchill died at his London home on January 24, 1965.

For More Information

Broad, Lewis. *Winston Churchill: A Biography.* 2 vols. New York: Hawthorne, 1963.

Churchill, Winston S. *Winston S. Churchill: His Complete Speeches, 1897-1963.* 8 vols. New York: Chelsea House, 1974.

Gilbert, Martin. *Winston Churchill.* 8 vols. Boston: Houghton Mifflin, 1988.

Humes, James C. *Churchill: Speaker of the Century.* New York: Stein & Day, 1980.

Nikita Khrushchev
1894-1971

Personal Background

A peasant child. Nikita Sergeyevich Khrushchev was born to peasant parents on April 17, 1894, in Kalinovka, a small and poor farming village on the Russian side of the border with Ukraine. It was difficult for a farmer to support a family in Kalinovka, so every autumn Khrushchev's father left the farm to work in the coal mine of the Ukrainian Donets Basin, three hundred miles to the southwest. As a boy Khrushchev helped with the family finances by tending sheep and cattle. There was not much time for formal education—just a couple of winters during which he attended the village school. Khrushchev, however, learned quickly, so this brief education made him better educated than the average child of Kalinovka.

Laborer. In 1908, when Khrushchev was fourteen years old, his father decided to leave the land for good and moved the family to Yuzovka, a company-owned town close to the mine where he worked each autumn. In the early twentieth century many of the mines and factories of Ukraine and other parts of the future Soviet Union were foreign-owned. A year after moving to Yuzovka, young Khrushchev went to work for the German Bosse Engineering Works as an apprentice fitter. He was still employed there in 1912 when a workers' strike began in a goldfield on the Lena River in Siberia. When the British owners violently put down the

▲ **Nikita Khrushchev**

Event: Moving toward the close of the Cold War.

Role: After Joseph Stalin's death in 1953, Nikita Khrushchev worked his way up to the top ranks of the Communist Party of the Soviet Union. Three years later, he delivered a speech at the Twentieth Party Congress that denounced Stalin and out-lined some of the horrors of the Stalin reign. In the years that followed, Khrushchev tried to maintain Soviet power throughout Europe and stabilize domestic economic conditions.

strike, sympathy strikes were organized all over Russia and Ukraine. Khrushchev took a small part in organizing the strike at Bosse and was fired for this action. However, by this time he was a skilled worker, and he quickly found other employment as a mechanic in a French-owned mine.

When World War I began, Khrushchev, like most mine workers, was exempt from the draft. During the war he was assigned to a machine shop that maintained equipment for several mines. In 1915 and 1916, he helped organize strikes among the miners, but there is no evidence that he had joined any revolutionary parties at that time. In fact, Khrushchev did not join the Bolshevik party (a group of extremists who led the Revolution of 1917, took over control of the Russian government, and formed the communist Soviet state) until 1918.

Civil war. The Bolsheviks were a minority party in the new Soviet Union, and their capture of power immediately led to the outbreak of civil war in 1919. Khrushchev served with the Red (Soviet) Army as a low-ranking officer in a supply unit. After the war, which left the Soviet Union and its industries in a shambles, he was appointed deputy manager of a mine operated by the Soviet government. Organized into labor units, the miners worked under appalling conditions, and Khrushchev's job was to bully them into restoring coal production to its prewar levels. From this position Khrushchev rose slowly but continuously. The government also provided him with more formal education. In 1922 he was chosen to study at the Don Technical College at Yuzovka.

The Khrushchev Family

In 1914, the year World War I began, Nikita Khrushchev married his first wife, Yefrosinya. Two years later the couple had a son, Leonid, and after two more years, a daughter, Ulia.

Rising through the ranks of the Communist Party. Khrushchev had begun his career as a Communist Party official in the early 1920s. By 1938 he had become a member of the Politboro, the Soviet Union's ruling "parliament," and the next year was named ruler of Ukraine and eastern Poland. During World War II, Khrushchev was an officer in the Soviet Army, ending the war as lieutenant general. By 1949 he was serving as first secre-

▲ Lavrenti Beria, Georgi Malenkov, K. E. Voroshilov, and Joseph Stalin in July 1949; Khrushchev challenged Malenkov and Beria for Soviet leadership when Stalin died in 1953.

tary of the Moscow City Party and secretary of the Soviet Central Committee in charge of agriculture.

Efficient party member. In all these positions, Khrushchev was unswerving in his effectiveness and in his loyalty to Joseph Stalin, the brutal leader who had become first secretary of the Communist Party in 1922 and would go on to take exclusive charge of the Soviet Union. Khrushchev efficiently led the purge (or removal) of Ukrainian nationalists (who challenged Stalin's rule), supervised the building of the Moscow Railway, and tried to initiate reforms in agriculture, which under Stalin had suffered greatly to pay for his expansion of heavy industry. More importantly for his own career, Khrushchev faithfully attended and spoke at party congresses, condemning anyone who opposed Stalin's plans. He frequently demanded "repressive measures" against these anti-Stalinists. In this way, he helped pave the way for the ruthless purges (removing unwanted members of government, military, and community groups, usually by imprisonment or execution) that Stalin felt necessary in order to bring the Soviet Union under his total command.

Even as a backer of Stalin, however, Khrushchev attempted to help farm workers. He proposed at one time the development of "agro-towns" to improve workers' living conditions. For this, Georgi Malenkov, one of Stalin's agricultural advisers, accused Khrushchev of "anti-Marxism"—of putting the welfare of the peasants ahead of the welfare of the state. Khrushchev was removed from his agricultural posts, but Stalin was not yet confident of his own power. Malenkov and Soviet defense expert Lavrenti Beria were powerful threats themselves, so Stalin gave Khrushchev control of the party organization as a sort of buffer against possible rebellion by the other two. Khrushchev was, therefore, in a position to challenge Malenkov and Beria for Soviet leadership when Stalin died in 1953.

In His Own Words: How Khrushchev Got Rid of Beria

Khrushchev led Communist Party leaders to condemn Lavrenti Beria, who was tried and found guilty of treason. Khrushchev later explained that this was done without any real proof of wrongdoing; he had only suspected that Beria wanted to seize power for himself. Therefore, according to Khrushchev, he and his cohorts "came to the unanimous decision that the only correct measure for the defense of the Revolution was to shoot [Beria] immediately. This decision was adopted by us and carried out on the spot" (Pryce-Jones, p. 49).

Participation: Moving Toward the Close of the Cold War

Head of the Soviet Union. In the struggle for power that followed Stalin's death, Malenkov—with the support of Beria—seemed at first to be getting the upper hand. Beria, however, had been involved with the Soviet secret police and active in Stalin's purges; he was feared and hated by almost everyone in the presidium (the communists' governing group). In July 1953 Khrushchev was successful in engineering Beria's removal and execution. After that, Malenkov's power was weakened and Khrushchev was able to install a government by a small group with himself at its head.

The Cold War. Between 1953 and 1956, acting heads of the Soviet Union began talks with Western powers to ease the Cold War that had developed at the end of World War II. (A cold war is

▲ Khrushchev addressing the United Nations General Assembly on October 3, 1960. When Khrushchev began to take control of the Soviet Union in 1956, he immediately began discussions aimed at ending the Cold War.

a condition of extreme political tension between nations that falls short of a military conflict.) Stalin's government had tried unsuccessfully to take over more of Germany. The Soviets further angered the West by giving vast war supplies to the Chinese communists. In addition, Stalin occupied Hungary and Romania and threatened Greece.

When Khrushchev began to take control of the Soviet Union in 1956, he immediately began discussions aimed at ending the Cold War. But the West had learned to distrust the Soviets under Stalin's rule. U.S. secretary of state John Foster Dulles, for one, was not willing to believe that the Soviets would change under Khrushchev, even though the new Soviet leader took great pains to announce to the world that his rule would be different.

The Twentieth Party Conference. At the Communist Party conference of 1956, Khrushchev presented a report that rocked the Soviet communists and the world: as the conference neared an end, he gave a twenty-thousand-word-long speech in which he denounced Joseph Stalin. Stalin, he said, had allowed his government to grow into a "cult of personality." That had resulted in distortion of the party principles—of democracy and revolutionary legality. Although Khrushchev had willingly served as a Stalin aide in the purges of his enemies, he now criticized the brutality and violence that reigned in the 1920s and 1930s. He described how Stalin's purges had resulted in the elimination of two-thirds of the 139 members of the Party Central Committee elected at the Seventeenth "Congress of Victors." Khrushchev also described the mass imprisonment of party workers and deportations of entire nationalities. He was announcing a major change in the government of the Soviet Union.

Reformist measures. Under Khrushchev's management, the push toward industrialization at the expense of agriculture was eased. The Soviet Union still strove to become a leading industrial nation, but with a mix of light industry added to Stalin's heavy industries. At the same time, the mighty Soviet army was reduced by more than a million soldiers. And, of course, the leadership of the Soviet Union broadened, now that it was governed by committee. Soviet citizens looked forward to greater food supplies and a little less government interference in their lives. Further supporting this new relaxed government, Khrushchev began to free thousands of political prisoners. As a result, inside the Union it looked as if there might be an easing of the Soviet government control. Among neighbors, however, Khrushchev's rule took on a different look.

Crushing rebellions in Poland and Hungary. In 1956, just before Khrushchev became premier of the Soviet Union, the world heard his anti-Stalin speech. The citizens of Poland then thought it was safe to stage a revolt against Soviet domination, but they were wrong. Khrushchev responded by appointing a new communist leader for Poland, Vladislaw Gomulka, and reassigning the Soviet army general in Poland. The situation was much worse in Hungary, where students and workers had also rebelled that same year. Khrushchev responded to the Hungarians with a brutal attack that swept the whole country. When his army had finished, all opportunity for Hungary to develop its own strategies under communism were gone; the people were even more oppressed under János Kádár, whom Khrushchev appointed to head the Hungarian communists.

Sputnik. A year after Khrushchev took office, the results of the Soviet emphasis on industry and technology began to show. In October 1957 the Soviets launched *Sputnik,* the first space satellite. The success of this launch did little to calm the fears of the Western world. In fact the United States and others panicked at their first jolting awareness of the progress in Soviet technology. Their fears increased later that year, when the Soviets launched the world's first atomic-powered ship, an ice-breaker called the *Lenin.*

Berlin Wall and other reactions to the West. In 1955 Khrushchev arranged a meeting with U.S. president Dwight Eisenhower. Five years later he scheduled another with incoming President John Kennedy. In both cases, the Soviet leader called the meetings to try to persuade Western powers that it was a mistake to allow Germany to grow prosperous and rearm. The Soviets had reason to be concerned—twenty million Soviet citizens had lost their lives in World War II, which had been started by the Germans. But neither U.S. president cared to listen.

The World Festival of Youth

In 1957 the Soviet Union once more showed a softer side to its international strategy. Moscow was opened to thirty-four thousand young foreigners who attended a two-week-long World Festival of Youth. Sixty thousand Soviet young people also participated in the festival.

By mid-1961 swarms of refugees were fleeing Soviet-occupied East Berlin for freedom in the democratic West. (The large city of Berlin, located in the former republic of East Germany, was itself divided into an eastern and western section. East Berlin was a designated communist area; West Berlin, occupied by Great Britain, France, and the United States, was noncommunist.)

Angry that the Americans would not listen to Soviet concerns, Khrushchev ordered a great wall to be erected separating East and West Berlin. The wall stood as a symbol of the Cold War until November 1989.

Nuclear threat. Later in 1961 the Khrushchev-led Soviet Union responded to cold-war-type actions by the United States. The Western Allies had installed missiles in Eastern Europe; these missiles were aimed at potential Soviet targets. The Allied action was the subject of Soviet protests in the United Nations. Around the same time, the United States was becoming increasingly concerned about communist leader **Fidel Castro**'s (see entry) rise to power in Cuba—and his close ties to the Soviet Union. Even a very small communist country such a short distance from American borders threatened the U.S. government. President John Kennedy authorized a plot—now known as the Bay of Pigs invasion—to invade Cuba and rid it of Castro.

The plot was disastrously unsuccessful. The next year tensions escalated between the United States and the Soviet Union after Khrushchev established Soviet missile sites in Cuba. A military confrontation was averted when Khrushchev agreed to remove the missiles if the United States ended its naval blockade of the island and pledged to reverse plans for an invasion of Cuba.

Aftermath

Economic development in the Soviet Union did not progress rapidly, however, and Khrushchev's own followers began to turn against him. When he announced in 1964 that the next "Five-Year Plan" would focus on producing consumer goods rather than more heavy industry, opposing politicians removed him from office. Leonid Brezhnev, a leading Communist Party official, then assumed control and tried to reorganize the Soviet Union along Stalinist ideas. The expense of his remodeling and military buildup would eventually lead to the bankruptcy of the Soviet Union.

Khrushchev spent much of the remainder of his life writing his memoirs. On September 11, 1971, he died of a heart attack in Moscow.

For More Information

Burlatsky, Fedor. *Khrushchev and the First Russian Spring*. Translated by Daphne Skillen. New York: Scribner's, 1991.

Frankland, Mark. *Khrushchev*. New York: Stein & Day, 1967.

Khrushchev, Nikita S. *Khrushchev Remembers*. Translated by Strobe Talbott. Boston: Little, Brown, 1970.

Khrushchev, Nikita S. *Khrushchev Remembers: The Last Testament*. Translated by Strobe Talbott. Boston: Little, Brown, 1974.

Medvedev, Roy. *Khrushchev*. Translated by Brian Pearce. New York: Anchor, 1983.

Pryce-Jones, David. *The Hungarian Revolution*. New York: Horizon, 1970.

Fidel Castro

c. 1926-

Personal Background

The Castros. Angel Castro Argis, a native of Lugo, Spain, had become acquainted with Cuba (an island in the Caribbean just south of Florida) when he was stationed there as a Spanish cavalry-man. In 1905 he succeeded in immigrating to the Americas. A big and powerful man, Angel found work in the Cuban nickel mines and began to save his money. He had no formal education but taught himself to read and write while he kept an eye out for oppor-tunities in the new world. He found them in the sugar industry.

Angel began to organize teams of farm workers to harvest the crops that supported the United American Fruit Company. With his earnings he gradually acquired bits of land and began his own cultivation of sugar crops. Eventually Angel Castro became a prosperous sugar contractor, but he vividly remem-bered the hardships of his early peasant existence and retained a cynical view of the world.

Fidel Alejandro Castro Ruz was the illegitimate son of Angel Castro Argis and Lina Ruz González. (Lina would later become Angel's second wife.) Castro was born on August 13—in either 1926 or 1927—on the Castro farm, "Las Manacas," near the town of Birán in the Oriente province of far eastern Cuba.

Education and life experience. Fidel Castro began formal schooling at the public school in nearby Marcane. Although the

▲ **Fidel Castro**

Event: Building a socialist state in Cuba.

Role: As a college student, Fidel Castro joined rebel forces intent on changing the Cuban government. He emerged as a key figure in the rebellion that overthrew the nation's dictator. Castro became the leader of Cuba in 1959.

Castro family lived comfortably in their large two-story farm-house, conditions at the local school reflected the plight of the region's farm laborers. Later, while in prison, Castro would recall this experience:

> My classmates, sons of humble parents, generally came to school barefoot and miserably clad. They were very poor. They learned their ABC's very badly and soon dropped out of school, though they were endowed with more than enough intelligence. They then foundered in a bottomless, hopeless sea of ignorance. (Castro in Bourne, p. 20)

When Castro was six years old, his parents decided to send him and two of his siblings to the city of Santiago de Cuba to live and study under the sister of their village school teacher. According to biographical sources, Castro never understood why the three youngsters were put on a train and sent away from home; the time he spent in Santiago de Cuba was sheer misery for him. Two years later, his parents enrolled him in La Salle School, a Catholic boarding institution. For the next decade, Castro would study in Catholic schools operated by Jesuit priests.

Castro's Birth Year

Among historians and biographers, there is much confusion about Castro's actual birth year. Fidel Castro himself seems not to care much about the exact date, but his older brother, Ramon, claims it was 1927. Sometime in Castro's adult life, however, newspaper and television interviewers began to take 1926 as the real birth year, and Castro went along with this date.

Castro's experiences at La Salle reinforced his observations on the rigid nature of class distinctions. Even though his family was moderately wealthy, they still bore the marks of their peasant class beginnings. Consequently, Castro was looked down on by some of the school's wealthier, city-bred students.

In 1942 Castro completed his studies at La Salle and enrolled in a preparatory school, the Jesuit-run Collegio de Belén. His experiences under these Jesuits were much more positive and nurturing. Members of the Spanish-based priestly order at the college respected intelligence and leadership, and Castro quickly established himself as an outstanding student. He earned top grades in his academic subjects while excelling in athletics. In

▲ Castro addressing the United Nations General Assembly in 1960; a year earlier he had taken over as Cuban Communist Party leader, commander of the armed forces, and prime minister.

1943 and 1944, he played basketball, baseball, and soccer and was named the best all-around athlete in Cuba. At the same time, he developed his speaking skills and distinguished himself as one of the school's top debaters. Castro's Jesuit education also helped in

199

his development of discipline. The Jesuit priests did not break Castro's spirit, but they did tame his hot temper and teach him the value of self-sacrifice and patience.

Castro's revolutionary streak. In 1945 Castro enrolled at the University of Havana to study law. The mid-1940s was a time of political turbulence in Cuba. Students and professors at Havana were rebelling against the Cuban dictatorship of Fulgencio Batista. Batista was an army sergeant who had taken control of Cuba, engineering the selection of four presidents before being elected himself in 1940. After his term expired, he continued to control the increasingly corrupt government of Cuba. Castro participated in several revolutionary organizations at the university—some of which he later would denounce—and took active part in preparing for the Cuban Revolution.

> ### Marriage
>
> In 1948 Castro married Mirta Diaz-Balart. The two honeymooned in New York City. It may have been there that Castro bought a copy of Karl Marx's *Das Kapital* and began to consider a Marxist future for Cuba. Fidel and Mirta would have one son, Fidel Castro Diaz-Balart, during their six-year marriage.

But his activity was not limited to Cuba. In 1947 Castro joined an unsuccessful expedition to oust Generalissimo Rafael L. Trujillo, the ruthless dictator of the Dominican Republic. The next year he participated in an uprising in Bogotá, Colombia. By that time, Castro was already in trouble with the Cuban government. He was known to be an active member of the Ortodoxo Party, a social democratic party opposed to Batista and his associates.

Participation:
Building a Socialist State in Cuba

Rebel activity at Moncada. Castro finished his law studies in 1950 and focused his attention on plans for a revolution. Such a revolution had been brewing since Batista took control of Cuba in a military coup (or overthrow of the existing government) in 1933. Castro's activities as a rebel organizer and fiery speaker soon made him a recognized leader in the Cuban Revolution. By 1953 he had gathered a strong anti-Batista following and decided it was time for action. He set his sights on the military barracks at Moncada. Backed by more than a hundred rebels, Castro laid out a careful plan for an attack on the barracks scheduled for the night of July 26, 1953.

"26th of July Movement." Batista blasted the rebel attempt. The attack was foiled and ended in retreat. Many of the rebels were then rounded up and killed. Castro was captured but saved from death because an old university acquaintance just happened to be in charge of the army unit that discovered him. He was later imprisoned, tried, and sentenced to fifteen years in prison.

Political winds in Cuba were highly changeable, however. After Castro was in prison for a year, it seemed better to the Batista regime not to make a martyr of the revolutionary leader; Castro, his brother Raul, and some of the other rebels were pardoned.

The Castro brothers then moved to Mexico to carry out the revolution in the safety of exile. They began to organize again for war with Batista—this time under the organizational name of "26th of July Movement." Within a year, this group had planned a strategy to conquer Cuba. They would gather a small force, enter Cuba in the Oriente province, and head for the mountains. From there, they would carry out guerrilla battles (hit-and-run type attacks) with federal troops, while enlisting the help of the peasants.

Eighty-two rebels were packed aboard a small ship—one that could comfortably sleep only eight—for the trip to Oriente. But once more the rebel plans went astray. They were supposed to land at a small dock and meet up with a group of fifty other rebels. However, the leader of that group was arrested by Batista soldiers early on the day of the landing, so support never arrived. In addition, the Cuban army had learned of their plans. Castro made a forced landing on the northern coast of the Oriente province on December 5, 1956. More than half the rebels were killed by Cuban naval and army forces over the next few days. But the Castros, Argentine doctor and revolutionary Ernesto "Che" Guevara, and a small band of their followers survived and made it into the hills, where they launched their guerrilla rebellion.

Pressure on Batista increases. Batista was alarmed. He first tried to defuse any peasant uprising by announcing that Castro had been killed. Then, on January 15, Batista suspended civil rights throughout Cuba. Two days later, Castro's rebel force attacked a small army post at La Plata, capturing much-needed weapons and medicines. Five days after that, the group ambushed a military patrol, injuring twelve soldiers.

Castro's talk of democratic reform stirred opposition to the dictatorial Batista regime. Having gained the support and confidence of the oppressed peasant population and the urban anti-Batista forces throughout Cuba, he stepped up his guerrilla activity. In January 1957 he carried his message to the foreign press, rallying Cubans to join him. By May he had built and trained a small army. The struggle between the rebels and the Cuban government's army of thirty thousand soldiers continued for more than a year. Castro gained even more exposure after submitting a statement of his plans for Cuba to a foreign magazine called *Coronet*.

> ### Castro as Author
>
> Castro's speeches and interviews were published in several volumes over four decades. Among them are *History Will Absolve Me; Fidel Castro Speaks; Revolutionary Struggle: 1947-1958;* and *Our Power Is That of the Working People.*

By January 1, 1959, Batista realized that he had lost support both inside and outside of Cuba. He fled to the United States. Castro then took over as Communist Party leader, commander of the armed forces, and prime minister. In 1976 he became president of the state council while maintaining his command of the military and the party.

It was not long before Castro began to nationalize all of Cuba's commercial activities and institute a massive land reform to provide land to the peasant farmers. Within a year the Castro government had taken over all the businesses previously owned by United States companies, the dominant business forces in Cuba. This move alienated American supporters. With crops diminished by the land redistribution and the revolution, and with the United States now refusing to buy Cuba's principle product, sugar, Castro turned to the Soviet Union for support, claiming that he had been a Marxist-Leninist all along and would remain one until he died.

▲ Castro throws the opening pitch in the Cuban National Baseball Amateur Series in Havana in 1965. Castro continued to control Cuba with an iron fist into the 1990s.

(Marxist doctrine is based on the theory that a revolution led by the working class will lead to a classless society. Leninist doctrine gives the party a leading role in directing the actions of the working class.)

U.S. diplomatic relations with Cuba deteriorated between 1959 and 1961. Cubans who had immigrated to the United States became convinced that it would be best to rid the island nation of Castro. In 1961 about fifteen hundred exiled Cubans, trained by the Central Intelligence Agency (CIA) and armed by the U.S. government, landed on the Bahía de Cochinas (Bay of Pigs), hoping to incite a revolution and overthrow the dictator. The Bay of Pigs invasion was quickly defeated by the Cuban army. The next year the Soviet Union installed missiles in Cuba. In one of the touchiest moments of the Cold War (a period of intense political tension between two powers—notably the United States and the Soviet Union—that stops short of actual military conflict), President John F. Kennedy locked horns with Soviet leader **Nikita Khrushchev** (see entry) and finally persuaded the Soviets to withdraw the missiles.

Meanwhile, Castro consolidated his hold on the Cuban government. He refused to hold elections as scheduled; he took personal charge of Cuban economics and foreign affairs; and, quietly, his opponents in Cuba disappeared—frequently killed by order of the government.

For many years Castro's Cuba struggled desperately to succeed as a socialist state. Castro always needed massive assistance from the Soviet Union to support his failed economic policies—policies that were further hindered by a powerful U.S. boycott. He continued in the 1970s to receive economic aid from the Soviets and to support communist causes throughout the world, including those in Angola and Ethiopia. In spite of this close association with communist governments, Castro claimed to be nonaligned in world politics and even became chairman of the Organization of Nonaligned Nations Movement in 1979.

In the early 1990s Castro continued to control Cuba with an iron fist. After the Soviet Union was dissolved, he looked to Russia for aid. That aid, too, disappeared. Cuba's economy was in a desperate condition and in need of foreign capital. Castro was forced to open his country to foreign trade and tourism and made other concessions to capitalism, but maintained his stand as a dictator and socialist.

For More Information

Bourne, Peter G. *Fidel: A Biography of Fidel Castro.* New York: Dodd, Mead, 1986.

Matthews, Herbert Lionel. *Fidel Castro: A Political Biography.* New York: Simon & Schuster, 1969.

Meneses, Enrique. *Fidel Castro.* New York: Taplinger, 1968.

Szulc, Tad. *Fidel: A Critical Portrait.* New York: Morrow, 1986.

Alexander Dubcek

1921-1992

Personal Background

Alexander Dubcek missed being born an American by just a few months. His father, Stefan, a carpenter, had immigrated to the United States from Slovakia in 1912 and became an American citizen in 1916. As a staunch socialist, he was appalled when the United States entered World War I in 1917. (Socialism is a political and economic system based on government control of the production and distribution of goods. It clashes with the American capitalistic tradition of private ownership and competition in a free market.)

Stefan Dubcek attempted to dodge the draft, was caught, and sent to jail. Upon his release, he settled in Chicago. There he met his future wife, Pavlina, whose political views were even more radical than his own. In the meantime, the collapse of the Austro-Hungarian empire had made their native Slovakia a free nation (soon to become part of the new Czechoslovak republic), and in 1921 Stefan and Pavlina returned home. Alexander, their second son, was born in Uhrovec that November.

In Slovakia, Stefan Dubcek aligned himself with the newly formed Czechoslovak Communist Party. Fired by enthusiasm for the Russian Revolution and the new Soviet state, the Dubceks joined an Interhelpo cooperative run by the International Workers Relief and in 1925 immigrated to Kirghizia, a Soviet republic in central Asia. After seven years there, Stefan moved the family to

▲ **Alexander Dubcek**

Event: The Prague Spring.

Role: In October 1967 Alexander Dubcek emerged as a strong leader in the quest for reform within the Czechoslovak Communist Party. As the reform movement broadened and gathered momentum, it alarmed the Soviet leadership. Soviet forces invaded Czechoslovakia in August 1968 and abruptly ended the country's brief experiment with what Dubcek called "communism with a human face."

Gorki, in eastern Russia, where he went to work at an American-built auto plant. Shaken by Soviet dictator Joseph Stalin's purges (removal of opposition, often by imprisonment or execution) and the terror gripping the Soviet Union, the Dubceks returned to Slovakia in 1938.

After Munich. As a result of the Munich Agreement of 1938 between Great Britain, France, Germany, and Italy, Czechoslovakia lost two-fifths of its territory to Germany. Stefan, Julius, and Alexander Dubcek joined the newly formed—and illegal—Slovak-based Communist Party. (In theory, communism is a social and economic system rooted in the collective, or communal, ownership of property and the eventual emergence of a classless society. But some communist states in Central and Eastern Europe and in Asia [notably the Communist Party of the Soviet Union; CPSU] became totalitarian in nature, with strict control invested in an all-powerful central government.)

Before German Nazi leader Adolf Hitler had divided Czechoslovakia, there had been only one Czechoslovak Communist Party, which like the country had been dominated by Czechs. The Slovak-based party that came into being during World War II possessed an independent-minded leadership unwilling to blindly follow Soviet-imposed policies. In 1944, at the urging of Czech leader Eduard Benes, Slovaks staged a two-month uprising before the Germany army moved in to occupy the country.

The Dubceks continued their resistance. Alexander and Julius served in a Slovak brigade, Julius was killed in action, and Alexander was wounded twice during the fight against the Nazis. After being imprisoned by the Slovak authorities, Stefan Dubcek spent the last year of World War II at the Mauthausen concentration camp.

Rising in the Communist Party ranks. After the war, Czechoslovakia was reunified and ruled by a National Front Coalition with substantial communist representation. (About 38 percent of the Czechs and Slovaks voted for communist representatives.) This arrangement lasted until February 1948, when, under the leadership of Clement Gottwald, the communists took complete control of the government. Czechoslovakia was then closely allied with the Soviet Union and would remain so, through the rule of Gottwald's successors, Antonin Zapotocky and Antonin Novotny. (Their successor, Dubcek, would break with the Soviet strictness, but remain under Soviet control until 1989.)

Dubcek went to work at a yeast factory in Trencin, but in 1949 he was offered a full-time Communist Party job, which he accepted as a temporary assignment. He ended up rising in the party ranks because of his managerial skills and political reliability. At the time, Dubcek seemed to have no political ambitions.

In 1951, in the midst of the Stalinist trials and purges, Dubcek was transferred to Bratislava, the Slovak capital, working for the Central Committee Secretariat. He was sent to Moscow (the Russian capital) in 1955 to attend the Higher Political School and over the next few years witnessed the political unrest that followed Soviet leader **Nikita Khrushchev**'s denunciation of Stalin's policies at the Twentieth Party Congress in 1956 (see entry). For several years after that, Dubcek continued to rise within the ranks of the Czechoslovak Communist Party.

An Unlikely Leader

Until the moment he challenged Communist Party first secretary Antonin Novotny—one of Stalin's followers—in 1968 and won, there was little to indicate that Dubcek possessed any leadership interest at all.

Participation: The Prague Spring

The making of a challenger. Dubcek's conflict with Novotny, whom he would eventually replace as party boss, began in the early 1960s. It originated from two sources of disagreement: the slow pace of de-Stalinization (a period of liberalization that followed the death of Stalin), for which Novotny showed no enthusiasm, and the party leadership's longstanding contempt for Slovak concerns. Slovak communists bore the brunt of the purges of the early 1950s, which had been initiated by Stalin as a means of removing any potential obstruction to Soviet domination of the communist regimes installed in Eastern Europe. Many Slovaks had been imprisoned, others (most notably Vladimir Clementis, Czechoslovakia's foreign minister after the communist takeover) had been executed.

After Khrushchev denounced Stalin in 1956, thousands of these purge victims had been quietly released from Czech jails

▲ Dubcek speaks with a chimney sweep outside of Communist Party headquarters in Prague in 1968. Dubcek's Action Program promised the citizens of Czechoslovakia all the liberties of a social democracy except the right to unlimited private property.

but had not been officially cleared of their charges. Moreover, the Kosice Agreement of 1945 had formed the basis for the postwar reunification of Slovakia and the Czech lands into a single republic. The extreme centralization of power under communism denied the Slovaks any say over their local affairs; the new constitution Novotny forced upon the country in 1960 centralized power even further.

Cautious opposition. Unable to challenge Novotny directly, Dubcek had to proceed cautiously. In the meantime Novotny was under pressure to imitate Khrushchev's limited program of de-Stalinization. It was this pressure that gave Dubcek his openings. In 1962 he participated in an investigation into the Stalinist purges. He later admitted that he was sickened by what he learned about secret police methods and illegal party activity.

Dubcek's information helped isolate Novotny by discrediting several of his high-ranking appointees within the party bureaucracy. In 1963 Dubcek managed to win election as first secretary of the Slovak-based Communist Party; it was from this base of power that he rallied the opposition against Novotny over the next four years.

Showdown. By the time the Czechoslovak Central Committee began its session in October 1967, Novotny had alienated a broad coalition of Slovak nationalists, economic reformers, and writers. At the committee meeting, Dubcek made a speech in which he protested the mistreatment of Slovakia and advocated the total separation of party and state. In the violent debate that followed, it became clear that the majority of members were in favor of Novotny resigning his post as the party's first secretary.

Action Program. On January 5, 1968, Dubcek replaced Novotny as first secretary of the Czechoslovak Communist Party and moved quickly to introduce economic and political reforms. The blueprint for Dubcek's intended changes—his Action Program—was made public on April 9. The program promised the citizens of Czechoslovakia all the liberties of a social democracy except the right to unlimited private property. It proclaimed the freedom of the press, of assembly, and of association, and the right of the nation's people to travel abroad freely. In addition, special efforts were to be made to ensure the complete rehabilitation of all victims of past repression.

To guarantee equality between Czechs and Slovaks, the new republic was to become a federation, and Slovaks were to be given greater representation in federal bodies from which they had been previously excluded. Dubcek proposed a thorough decentralization of economic management and the legalization of small-scale private enterprise. The Action Program document stopped short of promising a multiparty system of government, but the revival of the National Front, combined with freedom of the press, implied a move in this direction. The Czechoslovak people were

▲ **August 21, 1968, a Czechoslovak student waves a national flag while standing on a Soviet tank in Prague, shortly after the Soviets invaded the country.**

delighted with these newfound freedoms. They briefly celebrated during what came to be known as the "Prague Spring."

The anti-Soviet sentiment that surfaced in the newly unmuzzled press alarmed the Soviets. Dubcek had initiated "communism with a human face" but was still loyal to and dependent on the Soviet Union. Over the next six months, he made strenuous efforts to alleviate the Soviet government's concerns, but he failed in his attempts.

War games. Despite Dubcek's assurances that his reforms would not remove Czechoslovakia from the Soviet bloc (a united group of nations), the Soviet press considered them a "counterrevolution" designed to undermine communism and restore capitalism. Czechoslovakia then became the victim of military intimidation by Warsaw Pact troops (armies of the communist countries that had signed the Eastern European Mutual Assistance Treaty in 1955). Talks between Soviet and Czech leaders at Cierna in Slovakia at the end of July failed to produce any agreement.

Invasion. On the night of August 20, 1968, the armies of the Soviet Union, Hungary, Poland, East Germany, and Bulgaria crossed over into Czechoslovakia. Dubcek and his reformist allies were seized by Soviet troops and flown to Moscow. On the 28th, after his release and return to Prague, Dubcek went on television to tearfully plead for the nation's acceptance of the agreement dictated to him in Moscow.

Aftermath

Disgrace. Dubcek retained the title of party head until the following April, when he was replaced by turncoat reformer Gustav Husák. In the period of "normalization" that followed the invasion, reformers were ousted from party and government posts, and harsh censorship was reimposed. In May 1970, after a brief appointment as ambassador to Turkey, Dubcek was expelled from the party altogether. To avoid exile in the West, he returned home. He resettled in Bratislava and was assigned a menial job with the Forest Administration.

The Velvet Revolution. On December 3, 1989, after two weeks of massive demonstrations, the communist government surrendered power to the democratic opposition, led by a group known as the Civic Forum. The bloodless transfer of power became known as the Velvet Revolution. On December 29, Dubcek was elected speaker of the National Assembly. He died on November 7, 1992, after sustaining serious injuries in a car accident. On January 1, 1993, Czechoslovakia split into the Czech and Slovak republics.

For More Information

Dubcek, Alexander. *Hope Dies Last: The Autobiography of Alexander Dubcek*. Translated by Jiri Hochman. New York: Kodansha International, 1993.

Shawcross, William. *Dubcek*. New York: Simon & Schuster, 1970.

Bibliography

Aczel, Tamas, and Tibor Méray. *The Revolt of the Mind.* London: Thames & Hudson, 1961.

Allen, Jonathan. "A Long Road Home." *Command 24* (September-October 1993): 38-43.

Baldwin, James. *Go Tell It on the Mountain.* New York: Knopf, 1953.

Baldwin, James. *The Evidence of Things Not Seen.* Orlando, Florida: Holt, Rinehart & Winston, 1985.

Bonachea, Roland, and Nelson Valdés. *Revolutionary Struggle: The Selected Works of Fidel Castro.* Cambridge, Massachusetts: MIT Press, 1971.

Bonavia, David. *The Chinese.* New York: Lippincott, 1980.

Brendon, Piers. *Winston Churchill.* New York: Harper, 1991.

Castro, Fidel. *Fidel Castro Speeches.* 3 vols. New York: Pathfinder Press, 1981-85.

Chou, Eric. *Mao Tse-tung: The Man and the Myth.* New York: Stein & Day, 1980.

Cramlsjaw, Edward. *Khrushchev: A Career.* New York: Viking, 1966.

Ewen, David. *Book of Modern Composers.* New York: Knopf, 1950.

Fairbank, John King. *The Great Chinese Revolution: 1800-1985.* New York: Harper, 1986.

Flem, Penna Frank. *The Cold War and Its Origins, 1917-1960.* Garden City, New York: Doubleday, 1961.

Franqui, Carlos. *Diary of the Cuban Revolution.* New York: Viking, 1976.

Fryar, Peter. *Hungarian Tragedy.* London: Dobson, 1956.

Gilbert, Martin. *Churchill: A Life.* New York: Holt, Rinehart & Winston, 1982.

Gilbert, Martin. *Winston Churchill: The Wilderness Years.* Boston: Houghton, 1982.

Halperin, Maurice. *The Rise and Decline of Fidel Castro.* Berkeley: University of California Press, 1972.

Heilbron, Jacob E. "Stalin: The True Leninist." *Global Affairs 6,* no. 2 (Spring 1991): 132-53.

Hughes, Gwyneth, and Simon Welfare. *Red Empire—The Forbidden History of the USSR.* New York: St. Martin's, 1990.

Kerner, Robert Joseph. *Masaryk: A Memorial Address Delivered before the Czechoslovak Sokol of San Francisco on October 31, 1937.* Berkeley, California: University of California Press, 1938.

Khrushchev, Nikita S. *Khrushchev Speaks: Selected Speeches, Articles, and Press Conferences, 1949-1961.* Edited by Thomas P. Whitney. Ann Arbor: University of Michigan Press, 1963.

BIBLIOGRAPHY

Khrushchev, Sergei. *Khrushchev on Khrushchev: An Inside Account of the Man and His Era by His Son.* Translated by William Taubman. Boston: Little, Brown, 1990.

Leffler, Melvin P. *A Preponderance of Power: National Security, the Truman Administration, and the Cold War.* Stanford, California: Stanford University Press, 1992.

Macartney, C. A. *October Fifteenth: A History of Modern Hungary, 1929-1945.* 2 vols. Edinburgh, Scotland: Edinburgh University, 1961.

Mao Zedong. *Chairman Mao Talks to the People: Talks and Letters, 1956-1971.* Edited by Stuart Schram. New York: Pantheon, 1974.

Meyer, Carl Ernest, and Tad Szulc. *The Cuban Invasion: A Chronicle of Disaster.* New York: Praeger, 1962.

Nagy, Ferenc. *The Struggle behind the Iron Curtain.* New York: Macmillan, 1948.

Nagy, Imre. *On Communism: In Defense of the New Course.* London: Thames & Hudson, 1959.

Oppenheimer, A. *Castro's Final Hour.* New York: Simon & Schuster, 1982.

Potok, Chaim. *Wanderings: Chaim Potok's History of the Jews.* New York: Fawcett, 1980.

Quirk, Robert. *Fidel Castro.* New York: Norton, 1993.

Spielvogel, Jackson J. *Western Civilization.* 2nd ed. St. Paul, Minnesota: West, 1994.

Szulc, Tad. *Fidel: A Critical Portrait.* New York: Morrow, 1986.

Wheatcroft, Andrew. *The World Atlas of Revolutions.* New York: Simon & Schuster, 1983.

Index

Bold indicates entries and their page numbers; (ill.) indicates illustrations.

PROFILES IN WORLD HISTORY

Significant Events and the People Who Shaped Them